北京航空航天大學
BEIHANG UNIVERSITY

GLOBAL
BEIHANG
Go Global. Light the Future.

Study at Beihang, Light the Dream
Growth Stories of International Alumni

留学北航 点亮梦想
国际校友成长故事

北航国际合作部　组编

人民邮电出版社
北　京

图书在版编目（CIP）数据

留学北航 点亮梦想：国际校友成长故事 / 北航国
际合作部组编. -- 北京：人民邮电出版社，2025.
ISBN 978-7-115-67344-2

Ⅰ. G649.281

中国国家版本馆 CIP 数据核字第 2025A701W0 号

内 容 提 要

本书以"留学北航 点亮梦想"为题，讲述了 15 位来自全球不同国家的国际学生从初入北航的文化适应，到学术探索，再到职业发展的成长历程，如意大利学生保罗在双学位项目中取得学术突破，韩国学生金大洙从飞行器设计专业跨界转型自媒体，赞比亚学生田仁治依托北航技术优势创业并推进中非合作，德国学生托比亚斯在自旋电子领域取得关键性进展等。这些故事既是国际学生个人奋斗的缩影，也是北航推动高等教育国际化、服务"一带一路"倡议的生动注脚。

本书既是北航国际教育成果的见证，也是中外青年互学、互鉴的精彩展现，不仅为广大国际学生提供了留学北航的真实参考，更通过鲜活的案例传递了教育无国界、梦想无边界的理念。

◆ 组　　编　北航国际合作部
　　责任编辑　顾慧毅
　　责任印制　马振武

◆ 人民邮电出版社出版发行　　北京市丰台区成寿寺路 11 号
　　邮编　100164　电子邮件　315@ptpress.com.cn
　　网址　https://www.ptpress.com.cn
　　北京九天鸿程印刷有限责任公司印刷

◆ 开本：700×1000　1/16
　　印张：15.75　　　　　　　　2025 年 7 月第 1 版
　　字数：302 千字　　　　　　2025 年 7 月北京第 1 次印刷

定价：99.80 元

读者服务热线：(010)81055410　印装质量热线：(010)81055316
反盗版热线：(010)81055315

编委会

从北航启航，奔赴世界的精彩

1957 年 10 月，世界上第一颗人造卫星划破苍穹，成功发射，人类自此进入了探索宇宙、洞察地球的崭新时代。这一伟大创举，让人类对居住已久的星球有了更为系统、全面和深入的认知。然而，在探索自然奥秘、逐梦浩瀚星空、洞悉人类自身的漫漫长路上，我们仍需砥砺前行。教育，作为培育人才的摇篮，通过代代传承、持续深耕，推动着科技进步、社会发展，进而促进人类社会不断向前。

实践充分证明，国际人才流动是促进人才培养、推动地区与生源国科技发展的重要途径。回顾世界留学历史，不难发现，国际学生在选择留学目的地时，往往倾向于科技、教育、经济和文化都相对发达的国家。中国历史悠久，文明璀璨，在国际舞台上向来拥有举足轻重的文化影响力。随着改革开放的不断深入，中国实现了飞速发展，如今已稳坐世界第二大经济体的宝座，其发展理念、实践经验及科技成就举世瞩目。当全球的目光纷纷聚焦东方，"留学西方"的传统

格局正逐步向"留学东方"转变。作为东方大国,我们有充足的理由相信,来华留学事业必将迎来更为辉煌的明天。

自1993年北京航空航天大学(简称北航)开启对国际学生的培养工作,岁月的长河中便流淌着一个个动人的故事。从最初迎接18名国际学生的起步探索,到如今生源覆盖130多个国家、累计培养3000余名国际学生的蓬勃发展,北航国际学院就像一座汇聚多元文化的灯塔,吸引着不同肤色、不同文化背景的学子们在此相聚、交融、成长。

北航国际学生培养工作始终与国家外交大局紧密相连,积极响应国家政策,秉持"留学北航 点亮梦想"的美好愿景,坚持将学校的学科优势转化为国际学生的培养优势,把教学改革与创新实践转化为培养能力。在工作理念与方式上,力争实现从被动到主动、从管理到服务、从实干到巧干的转变。

随着中国在经济、科技、教育等领域的迅猛发展,以及"一带一路"倡议的有力推动,越来越多世界各地的学生慕名来到北航。他们怀揣着对知识的渴望,在这里学习先进技术,与来自不同国家的学生交流。同时,北航与众多知名企业携手开展定向培养项目,为企业"走出去"提供坚实的人才支撑。这些项目的毕业生凭借在北航积累的知识与技能,回国后在各自的岗位上发挥着重要作用,有力推动中国与毕业生所在国在经贸、科技等领域的合作,成为国际合作的重要纽带。

在学科建设方面,北航充分发挥自身优势,精心打造特色国际教育项目。以空间技术应用方向为例,北航依托深厚的学科资源,为全球不同国家培养了150多位硕士和博士研究生。这些国际学生在北航学习先进的空间技术知识,回国后成为推动所在国家空间技术发展的中坚力量,进一步提升了北航在相关学科领域的国际影响力。

在北航,国际学生不仅在学术的海洋中收获知识,更实现了自我的成长与蜕变。面对语言障碍、文化差异等诸多挑战,他们勇往直前,毫不退缩。在与中国师生的紧密合作中,他们不断提升专业能力,培养了跨文化交流能力和团队协作精神。丰富多彩的校园活动为他们提供了展示才华的舞台;他们结交了来自五湖四海的朋友,留下了无数美好的回忆。

本书是北航国际学生成长历程的生动记录。书中的每一个故事,都如同夜空中闪耀的星辰，散发着独特的魅力。来自意大利的保罗，凭借自身的努力，成为北京航空航天大学—米兰理工大学双学位项目的首位学生，在学术探索与文化交融中实现了自我突破；来自韩国的金大洙，从飞行器设计专业转型自媒体，用独特的视角讲述精彩的中国故事；来自法国的张浩成因对中华文化的热爱踏入北航，克服重重困难后在职场中大放异彩……他们的故事，满是挑战与机遇的交融、奋斗与坚持的印记、成长与收获的喜悦。

这些国际校友故事，充分体现了北航开放包容的学术氛围和卓越的教育品质。每一个故事，都是北航与世界交流合作的鲜活例证，是文明互鉴的美好篇章，也为北航的国际化发展注入源源不断的活力。

在此，我要向所有参与北航国际学生培养工作的老师致以最衷心的感谢。是你们为国际学生提供了优质的教育资源和无微不至的关怀，助力他们在北航这片沃土上茁壮成长。同时，我也要向所有北航国际校友送上最诚挚的祝贺。相信你们在北航的经历一定是人生中宝贵的财富，希望在未来的日子里，你们继续弘扬北航精神，在各自的领域中勇攀高峰，取得更加辉煌的成就。

愿本书成为一座沟通的桥梁，连接北航与世界，让更多人了解北航的国际教育，领略北航国际学生的独特风采，感受北航的魅力与活力。期待这些故事能激励更多国际学生选择北航，开启属于他们的精彩旅程，在北航这片充满机遇与挑战的土地上，追逐梦想，实现人生价值。

留学北航，点亮梦想，北航记忆，历久弥新。

时任北航国际合作部部长

2025 年 3 月

Set Sail from Beihang University, Head for the World's Splendor

In October 1957, the first artificial satellite in the word pierced the sky and was successfully launched, marking the beginning of a new era for humanity in exploring the universe and gaining insights into the Earth. This great feat has enabled humanity to have a more systematic, comprehensive, and in-depth understanding of the planet we have long inhabited. However, on the long journey of exploring the mysteries of nature, pursuing dreams in the vast universe, and understanding ourselves, we still have a long way to forge ahead with determination. Education, as the cradle for cultivating talents, has promoted scientific and technological progress and social development through continuous inheritance from generation to generation and in-depth exploration, thus facilitating the continuous advancement of human society.

Practice has fully proven that the flow of international talent is an important way to promote talent cultivation and drive the technology development of regions and source countries. A review of international education history reveals that international students often tend to prefer countries that are relatively developed in terms of science and technology, education, economy and culture when choosing a study-abroad destination. China, with its long-standing history, enjoys a high reputation globally. With the continuous deepening of reform and opening-up, China has achieved rapid development. Now, China has firmly established itself as the world's second-largest economy. Its development concepts, practical experiences, and scientific and technological achievements have attracted worldwide attention. As the global spotlight turns towards the East, the traditional pattern of "studying in the West" is gradually shifting to "studying in the East". As a major power in the East, we have every reason to believe that the cause of international students studying in China will embrace an even more glorious future.

Since 1993, Beihang University has been dedicated to nurturing international students, and numerous touching stories have emerged over the years. Starting with the initial exploration of admitting only 18 international students, Beihang University has witnessed remarkable growth with students from over 130 countries and the cumulative cultivation of more than 3,000 international students. The International School of Beihang University is like a lighthouse that converges diverse cultures, attracting students of different skin colors and cultural backgrounds to gather, blend, and thrive.

The cultivation of international students at Beihang University has always been closely linked to the overall situation of national diplomacy. Actively responding to national policies, it adheres to the beautiful vision of "Study at Beihang, Light the Dream", and persists in transforming the university's disciplinary advantages into advantages in international students cultivation, and turning teaching reforms and innovative practices into cultivation capabilities. In terms of work philosophy and methods, Beihang University strives to shift from passivity to initiative, from management to service, and from hard-work to smart-work.

With the rapid development of China in economy, science and technology, education, and the strong impetus of the Belt and Road Initiative, more and more students from all over the world are coming to Beihang University. They come with a thirst for knowledge, acquire advanced knowledge and technology here, and promote communication among people from different countries. At the same time, Beihang University has partnered with many well-known enterprises to carry out targeted training programs, providing solid talent support for enterprises to "go global". Graduates of these programs, quipped with the knowledge and skills accumulated at Beihang University, play crucial roles in important positions after returning to their home countries, strongly promoting cooperation between China and their home countries in economy, trade, science and technology, and serving as key bridges in international cooperation.

In terms of discipline construction, Beihang University gives full play to its own advantages and carefully creates distinctive studying-abroad education programs. Taking the field of space technology applications as an example, relying on its profound disciplinary resources, Beihang University has trained more than 150 master's and doctoral students for different countries around the world. These international students learn advanced knowledge in space technology at Beihang University and, upon returning home, become the backbone of the space technology development in their home countries, further enhancing Beihang University's international influence in related disciplinary fields.

On the campus of Beihang University, international students not only immerse themselves in academic knowledge but also achieve self-growth and transformation. Facing challenges such as language barriers and cultural differences, they move forward bravely without hesitation. Through close collaboration with Chinese teachers and students, they continuously improve their professional abilities and cultivate cross-cultural communication skills and teamwork spirit. The rich and colorful campus activities provide them with a stage to showcase their talents. Here, they forge friendships with peers from all over the world and create countless wonderful memories.

This book vividly records the growth journey of international students at Beihang University. Each story in the book is like a twinkling star in the night sky, exuding its unique charm. Paolo Cuciniello from Italy, through his own efforts, became the first student of Beihang University-Politecnico di Milano double-degree program, achieving a self-breakthrough in academic exploration and cultural integration. Kim Daesu from the Republic of Korea shifted from Aircraft Design to Social Media, telling wonderful Chinese stories from a unique perspective. Haocheng Zhang from France, driven by his love for Chinese culture, entered Beihang University. After overcoming numerous difficulties, he has shone brightly in the workplace. Their stories are filled with the interweaving of challenges and opportunities, the marks of struggle and perseverance, and the joy of growth and harvest.

These alumni stories fully demonstrate Beihang University's open and inclusive academic atmosphere as well as its excellent educational quality. Each story is a vivid footnote to Beihang University's exchanges and cooperation with the world, a beautiful chapter of cultural mutual learning, and also injects a continuous stream of vitality into the international development of Beihang University.

Here, I would like to express my heartfelt gratitude to all the teachers who have involved in the cultivation of international students at Beihang University. It is you who have provided high-quality educational resources and meticulous care for international students, helping them thrive on the fertile land of Beihang University. At the same time, I would also like to extend my sincere congratulations to all international alumni of Beihang University. I believe that your experiences at Beihang University must be invaluable assets in your lives. I hope that in the days to come, you will continue to carry forward the spirit of Beihang University, strive for the highest peaks in your respective fields, and achieve even more brilliant accomplishments.

May this book serve as a bridge of communication, connecting Beihang University with the world, enabling more people to understand Beihang University's international education, appreciate the unique elegance of Beihang University's international students, and experience the charm and vitality of Beihang University. It is expected that these stories will inspire more international students to choose Beihang University, embark on their wonderful journeys, and pursue their dreams and realize their life values on this land full of opportunities and challenges.

"Study at Beihang, Light the Dream", and the memories will remain ever fresh.

Jingnong Weng

Director, International Relations Department, Beihang University (at the time)

March, 2025

自 1993 年接收首批国际学生以来，北航已累计接收全球 130 多个国家的 3000 余名国际学生，帮助他们攻读博士、硕士或学士学位。这些学生来自不同的大洲，有着不同的文化背景，就读于不同的专业，但拥有一个共同且响亮的名字——北航校友。文明因交流而多彩，因互鉴而丰富。为了展示国际校友在全球各地、各领域的奋斗足迹和多彩人生，北航国际合作部特别制作"留学北航校友故事"系列栏目，并汇集成册。这些故事不仅展现了国际校友"北航基因"的传承，也是连接过去与未来、北航与世界的桥梁，更是北航这所高等教育学府不断提高自身全球影响力、吸引力，以及学生全球胜任力的生动体现。"Study at Beihang, Light the Dream"不仅是一句口号，更是北航国际教育的核心目标。本书一章一主角，一人一故事，于平凡之中见北航精神，于点滴之中涵养北航气质，展岁月之斑斓长卷，书青春之壮志雄词。品诸般经历，悟人生真意，传校园佳话，颂时代新思。

Since admitting its first batch of international students in 1993, Beihang University has conferred doctoral, master's, and bachelor's degrees to over 3,000 international students from more than 130 countries worldwide. These students come from various continents, bringing rich cultural backgrounds and studying in different majors. Despite their diverse origins, they share a common distinction "Beihang Alumni". Civilizations become richer and more colorful through exchanges and mutual learning. To showcase the achievements and vibrant lives of international alumni across diverse regions and fields, International Relations Department of Beihang University has specially created Beihang University International Alumni Stories series. These stories not only reflect the heritage of Beihang University DNA among international alumni, but also serve as a bridge connecting the past and the future, as well as Beihang University and the world. Furthermore, they vividly illustrate how this prestigious Chinese university is continually enhancing its global influence, campus appeal, and student competence on the international stage. "Study at Beihang, Light the Dream" is not only a slogan, but also the core goal of international education at Beihang University. Each chapter features a different protagonist, and each individual has his/her own story. We can perceive the spirit of Beihang University in the ordinary, and cultivate the unique charm of Beihang University in the bits and pieces of life. All these stories are compiled into a collection, which unfolds the colorful tapestry of time and captures the lofty aspirations of youth. We can savor a variety of experiences, understand the true meaning of life, pass on the good legends from campus, and inspire new ideas of the times.

谨以此书，献给在北航国际学院学习过和正在学习的国际学生，以及与他们并肩奋斗的老师们。

To all the international students who have studied or are studying at the International School of Beihang University, and to the dedicated teachers who have stood by their side.

目录 CONTENTS

From Italy to China, My Dream Sets Sail from Here

01

从意大利到中国，我的梦想从这里启航

保罗·库奇涅洛

保罗·库奇涅洛（Paolo Cuciniello），来自意大利，是一位电气工程师，也是一位才华横溢的作家。2017 年至 2019 年，保罗就读于北航电气工程专业并获得硕士学位。他的北航留学之旅犹如绚丽画卷，充满了机遇与挑战，学术能力的提升、文化的交融和个人的蜕变相互交织。

Paolo Cuciniello, from Italy, is an electrical engineer, and also a new prominent writer. From 2017 to 2019, he pursued a master's degree in electrical engineering at Beihang University. His study journey at Beihang University was filled with opportunities and challenges, intertwined with academic ability growth, cultural exchange, and personal transformation.

扫码观看
采访视频

留学缘起

我叫保罗·库奇涅洛，来自意大利小镇——吉内斯特拉（Ginestra），一个历史悠久、文化底蕴深厚的地方。我在家乡起伏的山丘和充满活力的社区中长大，从小就对世界充满了好奇，尤其对科技类的事物和讲故事表现出浓厚的兴趣，这让我在同龄人中显得与众不同。当其他孩子沉浸在游戏中时，我却喜欢摆弄小工具，喜欢撰写自己的故事，这促使我后来走上了工程师和作家的双重职业道路。

真正激发我对亚洲，尤其是对中国的向往的是一种看似无形的东西，或许是马可·波罗的冒险故事在长辈们的低声细语中流传，或许是古代丝绸之路的魅力激发了我的想象，我感觉中国一直在召唤我，等待我去探索。

当我在米兰理工大学的学术旅程接近尾声时，我发现自己站在一个十字路口，面临着可能深刻影响未来的选择。这时，一个独特的机会出现了，它完美契合了我长期以来的兴趣，于是我决定去北航学习。内心深处，我一直渴望体验中国的文化和技术，而米兰理工大学与北航之间一项开创性的合作项目为我提供了一个难得的学术冒险机会。我感觉命运已经为我开辟了一条道路，我迫不及待地踏上征程。

我满怀期待又有些忐忑地登上了飞往中国的飞机。落地后，我受到了北航同学的热情迎接，他们真挚的笑容和热情的问候如阳光般驱散了我的陌生感和孤独感。到校后我惊喜地发现，北航为新生们安排了周到而温馨的迎新服务，报到流程井井有条。在米兰结识的中国同学也一直陪伴我左右，给予我帮助，让我在开启全新未知的旅程时，感受到了家一般的温暖。

学术探索之旅

初至北航，我被既具有挑战性又令人兴奋的学术氛围所包围。项目的后续课程设置丰富多样，理论知识既有深度又有广度，让我收获颇丰。在实验室里，我体验到了理论与实践结合的魅力，通过动手实验和操作，我对曾经那些晦涩难懂的理论知识有了更深刻的理解。北航的教授们在我的适应和成长中扮演了至关重要的角色，其中对我影响最深的是我的导师王少萍教授，她不仅在学术上给予我宝贵的指导，在生活等各方面都提供了珍贵的支持。她对学生的奉献超越了课堂，从一开始她就明确表示，她的办公室永远向学生敞开，随时为学生提供帮助。这种真诚的承诺让我感到安心，并赋予了我更多面对挑战的勇气。王教授与来自米兰理工大学的皮尼亚里教授共同塑造了我的学术品格，他们的教导培养了我的自信，使我能够坚定地探索新的学术领域。

保罗（右）和导师王少萍教授

我的同学们也是我在北航学习经历中不可或缺的一部分。我们的友谊建立在相互尊重和对卓越的共同追求之上。我们背景不同，但有共同的目标。我清晰地记得，课后我们常常聚在一起进行热烈的讨论，不仅分享学术见解，还交流文化故

参加组会，与导师同学交流讨论

事。这些交流丰富了我对世界的理解，开阔了我的视野。除了学术和文化交流，我们还会一起在食堂用餐，一起探索北京繁华的街道，抑或周末到附近的城市旅行。随着时间的推移，校园里的友谊变成了终身的联结。我时常与许多以前的同学和教授联系，这可以证明我们在学校里建立的情谊非常深厚。这些联结不仅丰富了我的个人生活，还为我打开了全球范围内的职业机会之门。

文化融入

在中国的生活不仅仅是一段学术旅程，更是一次深刻的文化融入，它重塑了我对世界的理解。踏入北京的那一刻起，我就沉浸在一个与以往完全不同的环境中。文化适应从认识语言、习俗、社交习惯等的细微差异开始，这既令人兴奋，又令人胆怯。我发现，以好奇和尊重的态度拥抱这些差异，我能够跨越最初的障碍，与中华文化建立更深的联系。

记得在春节期间，我的同学邀请我回他家过年，让我亲身感受这一重要文化活动。在体验这些新奇的习俗时，尽管远离家乡，我依旧感到了一种深深的归属感。此外，在中国各地的旅行进一步加深了我对中华文化丰富性和地理多样性的欣赏。从上海高耸的摩天大楼到桂林宁静的山水，每一个目的地都带给我新的体验。

保罗（右）和余华先生（摄影师：Antonino Benigno）

职业发展之路

毕业后，我站在了人生的十字路口，面临职业发展的抉择。幸运的是，国际交流的背景让我得到了两份充满机遇与挑战的工作。我在一家国际公司担任工程经理，这份工作要求扎实的专业知识与出色的管理能力，北航的学习经历为我提供了专业基础与国际视野，帮助我在职场竞争中脱颖而出。与此同时，在中国的旅程激发了我对写作的热情，我成了一名作家。在中国丰富的经历和遇到的各种故事为我的写作提供了独特的素材和灵感，而我的学术经历为我的叙事增添了深度，我将专业知识与创造性叙事相结合，这一组合引起了跨国读者的共鸣。

北航卓越的声誉和高质量的教育水平为我带来了独特的工作机会。在求职面试和工作社交中，简历上"北京航空航天大学"的字样给我的潜在雇主和合作伙伴注入了信心。在北航的学习经历也让我学会如何在不同文化背景下开展工作，与不同国家和地区的人合作，适应各种复杂的工作环境，并灵活应对各种挑战和变化。这种适应能力成为我在职场取得成功的关键因素之一。

个人成长与蜕变

在北航的经历以我从未想象过的方式深刻影响了我的生活和职业发展。北航是我成长的基石，为我提供了一个充满多样性的教育平台，这里不仅培养了我的专业技能，还让我深刻认识到跨文化交融和终身学习的重要性。

在中国的这段经历，促成了我的一次全面蜕变，我变得更加坚韧和自信，能够从容面对生活中的各种困难和挫折。在中国的传统文化中，我领悟到了一种平衡与和谐的生活态度，这种态度让我不再一味地追求速度和忙碌，而是学会了在适当的时候停下来，审视自己的内心，感受生活的美好。回顾这些经历，我充满感激，感谢有机会沉浸在一个既深厚又创新、既传统又充满活力的文化中。

对国际学生的建议

对于考虑未来要在中国学习的国际学生，我的建议简单而深刻：请以开放的心态拥抱机会。这段经历将为你带来挑战，拓宽你的视野，并以无数方式丰富你的生活。请准备好不仅要从课堂中学习，还要从文化和环境中学习。让这些经历塑造你，挑战固有观念，并帮助你在意想不到的维度上成长。

中国提供了传统与前瞻性创新的独特融合，是极佳的学习和成长之地。要充分享受这个充满活力的环境，抓住其提供的机会。这是一段发现之旅，它带来的回报远不止学术成就。

导师寄语

　　作为北京航空航天大学—米兰理工大学双学位项目的首位学生，保罗同学在北航学习期间，展现出了非凡的才能与学术潜力。在工程领域，他积累了扎实的专业知识；在跨文化环境中，他表现出了极强的适应能力和团队合作精神。凭借优秀的学业成绩和专业技能，他获得了课题组师生的一致认可。

　　这段学习经历无疑为他的职业生涯奠定了坚实基础，并为他未来的发展提供了重要的支持。作为他的导师，我倍感欣慰。他勤奋、谦虚、专注的品质，使他能够不断突破自我，在学习和工作中持续取得进步。我相信，无论在工程领域还是写作方面，保罗都将继续发挥他的才华，成长为多才多艺、富有创新精神的优秀人才。我期待着未来他能取得更优异的成绩。

导师简介

　　王少萍，北航自动化科学与电气工程学院教授，博士生导师，致力于机电控制、故障诊断、健康管理、可靠性与医工交叉的应用研究，是国家级领军人才，享受国务院特殊津贴专家，中国青年科技奖获得者、首批教育部新世纪优秀人才、北京市优秀教师、工信先锋、北京市"三八"红旗奖章获得者、北京市高校优秀共产党员、北京市巾帼创新之星和北京市优秀青年骨干教师。担任中国航空学会机电分会副主任委员、中国航空学会导航制导与控制分会委员、中国机械工程学会流体传动与控制分会常务委员、《北京航空航天大学学报》副主编、《航空学报》等多个国际杂志的编委。出版著作 4 本；发表学术论文 300 余篇，其中 SCI 收录100 余篇，EI 收录 200 余篇。

Fated at Beihang University

My name is Paolo Cuciniello, and I am from the quaint town of Ginestra, Italy, a place rich in history and culture. Growing up amidst the rolling hills and the vibrant communities of my hometown, I was imbued with a sense of wonder about the world, especially exhibited a keen interest in both technology and storytelling from a young age, which often set me apart from my peers. While other children were losing themselves in games, I found joy in tinkering with gadgets and penning my own stories. This dual fascination would later blossom into my dual career paths as an engineer and a writer.

What really sparked my curiosity toward Asia, China in particular, was something seemingly intangible. Perhaps it was the vibrant stories of Marco Polo's adventures shared in hushed whispers by elders, or the allure of the ancient Silk Road that inspired my imagination. It felt as though China was always calling me, waiting me to explore.

As I reached the latter stages of my academic journey at the Politecnico di Milano, I found myself at a crossroads with choices that could significantly shape my future. It was at this moment that a unique opportunity emerged, captivating my long-standing interest in China—I decided to pursue my studies at Beihang University. Internally, there was this persistent desire to connect with the culture and technology in China. Externally, the exciting announcement of a pioneering collaboration between Politecnico di Milano and Beihang University presented a rare opportunity for an academic adventure that would offer unparalleled insights and experiences. It felt like fate had opened a path on which I was eager to embark.

I boarded the plane to China with great anticipation and some apprehension. Upon arriving in Beijing, I was welcomed by the sincere smiles and warm greetings of my fellow students, which quickly eased my sense of unfamiliarity. Once I got to the university, I was pleasantly surprised by the thoughtful and well-organized orientation activities for newcomers. The registration process was smooth and efficient, and the Chinese classmates I had met in Milan were always there to assist me, making me feel the warmth and hospitality like a gentle spring breeze.

A Journey of Academic Discovery

The initial days at Beihang University were a whirlwind of new experiences, as I was enveloped by an academic environment that was both challenging and exhilarating. The courses offered were diverse, providing a depth and breadth of theoretical knowledge that greatly enriched my learning experience. Hands-on activities in the laboratory deepened my understanding of theories that had once seemed obscure. My professors at Beihang University played a crucial role in my adaptation and growth. One of the most profound influences was my supervisor, Professor Shaoping Wang, who not only guided me academically but also offered invaluable support and mentorship. Her dedication to her students extended beyond the classroom, and she made it clear from the first day that her office is always open for any guidance or assistance that students need. This genuine commitment was reassuring and empowered me more courage to take on challenges. Professor Wang, alongside Professor Pignari from Politecnico di Milano, shaped my academic character. Their mentorship fostered a sense of self-assurance that allowed me to navigate new academic terrains with determination.

My classmates, too, were an integral part of my experience at Beihang University. The friendships formed were built on mutual respect and a shared drive to excel. Though we have diverse backgrounds, we shared a common goal of learning and growing. I remember vividly the numerous occasions when my classmates and I gathered after lectures to delve into spirited discussions, sharing not just our academic insights but also our cultural stories. These exchanges enriched my understanding of the world, offering perspectives that were previously unknown to me. Beyond the academic and cultural exchange, we would also enjoy meals together in the university cafeteria, explore the bustling streets of Beijing, or take weekend trips to nearby towns. Over time, friendships on campus evolved into lifelong connections. I remain in touch with many of my former classmates and professors, a testament to the deep-seated ties forged during my time at school. These bonds have not only enriched my personal life but have continued to open doors to professional opportunities across the globe.

Cultural Immersion

Living in China was more than an academic journey. It was a profound cultural immersion that reshaped my understanding of the world. From the moment I set foot in Beijing, I was thrust into a totally different environment. The cultural adaptation began with the nuances language, customs, social interactions, which is both exhilarating and, at times, daunting. I found that by embracing these differences with a spirit of curiosity and respect, I was able to transcend initial barriers and connect more deeply with Chinese culture.

I vividly remember my classmate inviting me to his home during the Chinese New Year, offering a firsthand glimpse into this significant cultural event. As I participated in these intriguing rituals, I felt a deep sense of belonging despite being far from home. Additionally, my travels within China further deepened my appreciation for its cultural richness and geographic diversity. From the towering skyscrapers of Shanghai to the serene landscapes of Guilin, each destination offered new experience.

Career Paths

Upon graduating, I found myself at a crossroads in life, facing an important career decision. Thanks to my background in international exchange, I was fortunate enough to be presented with two promising career paths, each brimming with opportunities and challenges. On the one hand, I secured a position as an engineering manager at an international company, a role that required both technical expertise and strong management skills. On the other hard, my educational background at Beihang University provided me with a distinct advantage in this competitive job market. Simultaneously, my journey in China allowed me to explore my passion for writing, leading to a fulfilling career as an author. The rich experiences and the array of stories I encountered in China provided a unique tapestry of material and inspiration for my writings. My academic experiences added depth to my narratives, enabling me to integrate technical expertise with creative storytelling—a combination that resonated with readers across borders.

Beihang University's outstanding reputation and high-quality education have provided me with unique job opportunities. During job interviews and professional networking, the mention of Beihang University on my CV instilled confidence in potential employers and partners. My study experience at Beihang University also enabled me to learn how to work under different cultural backgrounds, collaborate with people from various countries and regions, adapt to all kinds of complex working environments, and respond flexibly to various challenges and changes. This adaptability has become one of the key factors for my career success.

Personal Growth and Transformation

I realize that the experiences I had at Beihang University have profoundly influenced my life and career in ways I could have never imagined. Beihang University served as a cornerstone for my growth, providing an educational platform that was rich in diversity. This environment not only cultivated my professional skills but also instilled a deep appreciation for cross-cultural engagement and lifelong learning.

The experiences in China have marked a profound personal transformation. I've become more resilient and confident, better equipped to face life's challenges and setbacks. From China's traditional culture, I have learned a life attitude of balance and harmony. This attitude has kept me from blindly pursuing speed and busyness and also taught me to stop at the right time to examine my inner self and feel the beauty of life. Reflecting on these experiences, I am filled with gratitude for the opportunity to have immersed myself in a culture that is both profound and innovative, traditional and dynamic.

Advice for International Students

To international students considering studies in China, my advice is simple yet profound: Embrace every opportunity with an open heart and mind. The experience will challenge you, broaden your perspectives, and enrich your life in innumerable ways. Be ready to learn not just from the classroom but from the culture and the environment. Allow these experiences to shape you, to challenge preconceptions, and to foster growth in unexpected dimensions.

China offers a unique blend of ancient tradition and forward-thinking innovation, making it an extraordinary place to study and grow. Please engage fully with this vibrant setting and the opportunities it presents. It is a journey of discovery that promises to reward far beyond the academic.

Message from the Supervisor

As the first student of the Beihang University-Politecnico di Milano dual degree program, Paul has demonstrated extraordinary talent and academic potential during his studies at Beihang University. In the field of engineering, he has accumulated solid professional knowledge, and in a cross-cultural environment, he has shown remarkable adaptability and teamwork spirit. With his excellent academic performance and professional skills, he has gained unanimous recognition and praise from both teachers and students in our research group.

His study experience has undoubtedly laid a solid foundation for his career and provided crucial support for his future development. As his supervisor, I am deeply gratified. His qualities of diligence, humility, and focus enable him to continuously push his boundaries and achieve progress in both study and work. I believe that whether in engineering or in writing, Paul will continue to leverage his talents and become a versatile and innovative individual. I look forward to seeing him achieve greater accomplishments in the future.

Introduction to the Supervisor

Shaoping Wang is a professor and doctoral supervisor at the School of Automation Science and Electrical Engineering, Beihang University. She is committed to electromechanical control, fault diagnosis, health management, reliability, and applied research in the intersection of medicine and engineering. She is a national leading talent, an expert enjoying special government allowance from the State Council, a recipient of the China Youth Science and Technology Award, one of the first batch of Excellent Talents in the New Century of the Ministry of Education, an Outstanding Teacher in Beijing, an Industry and Information Technology Pioneer, a recipient of the "March 8th Red Banner" Medal in Beijing, an Outstanding Communist Party Member in Beijing's universities, a Star of Women's Innovation in Beijing, and an Outstanding Young Backbone Teacher in Beijing. She serves as the deputy director of the Electromechanical Branch of Chinese Society of Aeronautics and Astronautics (CSAA), a member of the Navigation, Guidance, and Control Branch of CSAA, an executive member of the Fluid Power Transmission and Control Branch of the Chinese Mechanical Engineering Society, an associate editor of the *Journal of Beijing University of Aeronautics and Astronautics*, and an editorial board member of multiple international journals, such as *Chinese Journal of Aeronautics*. She has published 4 academic works and more than 300 academic papers, among which more than 100 are indexed by SCI and more than 200 are indexed by EI.

02

从飞行器设计到自媒体，我是
"韩国大猪哥"

北京航空航天大学

金大洙

　　金大洙（Kim Daesu），一位来自韩国的青年才俊。2016 年，他怀揣着对航空航天的热爱与憧憬，踏入了北航，成为飞行器设计与工程专业的一名国际本科生。在 4 年学习生涯中，他不仅在学术上追求卓越，还积极参与学校的各种活动，不断拓展自己的"朋友圈"。2020 年，金大洙本科毕业，开启了绚丽的人生新篇章。他涉足多个领域，在求索中不断挖掘自己的爱好和优势。恰逢中国自媒体行业蓬勃发展的黄金时期，他在这个领域展现出了无尽的活力与创造力，用青春磅礴的笔力，书写人生美丽的相遇。他运营的"韩国大猪哥"自媒体账号，在抖音、哔哩哔哩等社交平台上拥有数十万粉丝，总播放量达到数百万次。

　　Kim Daesu is a talented young man from the Republic of Korea. In 2016, driven by his passion and ambition for aerospace, he enrolled at Beihang University as an international undergraduate in Aircraft Design and Engineering program. During his 4 years of study, he not only excelled academically but also actively participated in various campus activities, constantly expanding his social circle. Kim graduated in 2020 and embarked on a new chapter in his life. After graduation, he ventured into divers fields, continuously defining his understanding of his passion and strengths through hands-on exploration. Happen to be in the prime period when the Chinese social media industry was booming, he demonstrated boundless vitality and creativity, in this field using the powerful strokes of his youth to write about the beautiful encounters of his life. His account, Korean Brother DAZHU, boasts hundreds of thousands of followers on platforms like Douyin and Bilibili, with millions of views in total.

扫码观看
采访视频

逐梦北航

　　我自幼就对飞机等飞行器充满了浓厚的兴趣。由于父亲的工作调动，我随他一起来到北京，有机会更加深入地感受中国的教育体系。在此过程中，北航这所在航空航天领域有着卓越地位的高等学府深深地吸引了我。北航拥有先进的教学设施、优秀的师资力量和丰富的学术资源，为学子们提供了广阔的发展空间。于是，我毅然决然地选择了北航，踏上了这段充满挑战的求学之旅。

　　初来中国时，我的汉语水平仅限于几句简单的问候，比如"你好""谢谢"等。但我深知语言是融入新环境的关键，所以下定决心要攻克语言关。我首先在北京师范大学进行语言学习，通过系统的课程学习，加之与老师、同学的深入交流，我的汉语水平迅速提高。不久，我便达到了国际学生报考北航本科要求的汉语水平。

　　刚进入北航的时候，全中文授课的环境对我来说是一个巨大的挑战。大一那年，语言障碍如影随形，老师的授课内容对我来说犹如天书。为了克服这一困难，我付出了极大的努力。课后，我会对着书本一字一句地查阅工具书，标注读音和翻译，反复地复习课本内容。我还会主动向中国同学请教，他们热情地给予我帮助和支持，耐心地为我解答问题，帮助我逐渐适应学习环境。我会主动与中国朋友一起聊天，参加活动，在实际情境中加深对汉语的理解与运用。通过这种方式，我的汉语水平提升了很多。到了大二，我终于能够听懂老师的专业授课了，我非常开心，仿佛拨云见日。那段时间真的很不容易，但正是因为努力和坚持，我才能够在求学的道路上迈出这坚实的一步。

　　我最钟爱的课程是飞行器结构设计。在这门课程中，我不仅

和同学们在一起

深入学习了飞行器的结构原理和设计方法，还通过实际案例和项目实践，培养了自己的创新思维和解决问题的能力。完成这门课程的学习后，我还与中国同学携手参加了飞机模型设计大赛，斩获佳绩。这次比赛不仅使我巩固了专业知识，还增进了我与中国同学之间的友谊，培养了我强烈的团队合作意识。

　　在北航的日子里，我的收获远不止这些。我汲取了丰富的知识，掌握了专业的技能，还结识了众多挚友，尤其是那些我可爱的中国朋友们。他们在我的学习和工作中，给我提供了无私的帮助和支持，成为我留学时光中最宝贵的财富。我参加过校园歌手大赛，虽然止步于复赛，但这段经历却让我结识了许多中国朋友。在社团活动中，我们一起排练，一起演出，共同度过了许多快乐时光。这些经历让我感受到了北航丰富多彩的校园文化，也让我的留学生活变得更加充实和有意义。

参加北航校园歌手大赛

　　更重要的是，我学会了如何与人相处，如何进行团队协作。这些经历让我变得更加成熟和自信。然而，我也有些许遗憾。初来北航时，我成绩优异，对本科学习充满信心。但大一那年，我未能全力以赴地学习，错失了许多提升专业成绩的机会。大一结束时的成绩单让我如梦初醒，意识到自己需要迎头赶上。于是我奋发图强，最终未负韶华。如果时光能够重新来过，我一定会在大一那段时间交上令自己、老师和母校更加满意的答卷。

　　在 2021 年回校参加毕业典礼时，我在社交媒体上写道："人生最美好的时光——我的学生时代结束了。特别感谢母校邀请我们 2020 届学生参加毕业典礼。去年由于疫情我们只举办了线上的毕业典礼，今天能够来到现场，站在北航的操场上参加毕业典礼，让我回想起幸福的学生时代。在本科四年的时间里，我虽然是国际学生，但和中国同学建立了十分深厚的情谊。生活方面，中国同学教给我许多有关中华文化的知识，丰富了我的见闻，加

老主楼前拍毕业照

深了我对中国的理解；学习方面，他们给予了我很多帮助，让我顺利地完成了学业。"

进入社会后，我总是很怀念跟同学们在一起的幸福时光。我想和我的大学同学们说："毕业快乐，希望某一天我们能够再见面。"我现在依然在中国工作，也是因为我的大学同学们让我对中国情有独钟。

"国际学院"四个字对国际学生来说是非常特殊的。我对国际学院老师的印象非常深刻。我记得负责教务工作的张艳老师，她对与工作相关的事务要求很严格，但平时在办公室遇到她时，又觉得她非常和蔼、善良。辅导员柳旭老师对我的帮助也很大。让我至今最难以忘怀的，是我的毕业设计指导老师——航空科学与工程学院的王吉东老师，我们到现在都一

参观北京航空航天博物馆

直保持联系。2020 年，我的毕业答辩只能在线上完成。在这个过程中，王老师给予了我莫大的指导与帮助，犹如一盏明灯照亮了我的前行之路。王老师不仅在学术上给予我专业的建议和指导，还关心我的生活和未来规划。我非常感激王老师的悉心教导，他是我人生中的重要导师，对我的成长和发展产生了深远的影响。

意外的美好转折

我一直都有一个在大学毕业后创业的梦想。然而，这个计划受到了疫情的影响。疫情过后我重回中国时，一个正在抖音实习的中国同学给了我一个建议，他觉得我可以尝试做自媒体，在互联网寻找创业的机会。一开始，我并没有太多的想法和计划，只是想着先试试看。我尝试在社交媒体上分享自己的生活、故事和见解，渐渐地吸引了一些粉丝。我发现自媒体不仅可以让我表达自己的

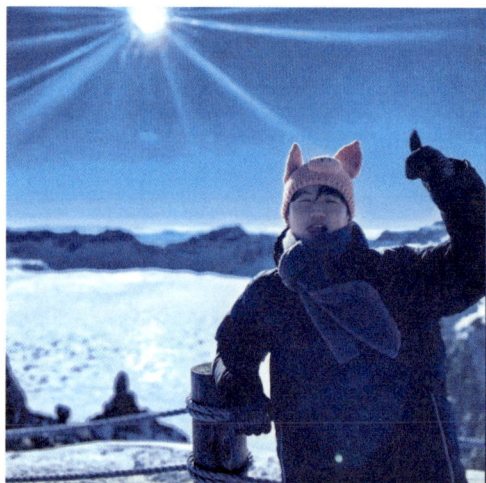
在外拍摄创意视频

想法和观点，还可以让我与更多的人交流和互动。我的第一条视频是 2021 年拍摄的关于新疆炒米粉的，当时我还不太会拍摄，也不会剪辑，只好边学习边工作。视频发布时我并没有特别期待会有很多人观看，但播放量却比想象的多。

刚开始在外面拍视频时，总会有人好奇地过来问我在干什么，我会感到很不好意思，表现也不自然，甚至不知道面对镜头该说些什么。在公共场合拍摄时，我也会遇到工作人员过来询问或阻止。有时候，我跑到很远的城市，想去某一家餐馆探店，结果却吃了闭门羹，不得不临时想办法拍摄其他素材。虽然遇到的困难很多，但我都一一克服了。现在，即使有粉丝进入镜头打招呼，我都能应对自如，也更加熟悉剪辑和运营的工作。在延边拍摄的《韩国小伙在延边初体验》这条视频，当时播放量达到了百万次，这让很多人认识了我。

自媒体平台首页

于是，我决定将自媒体作为自己的事业，开始了我的自媒体创业之旅。虽然这段旅程充满挑战，但我相信，只要我坚持下去，就一定能够实现自己的梦想。

作为一名美食博主，如果让我在北航拍摄一期美食视频，我绝对会推荐学院路校区的学五食堂。那里的饭菜种类繁多，口味绝佳，每一次去我都能大快朵颐。食堂宽敞明亮，干净整洁，让人用餐时心情都格外愉悦。我很期待能有机会回母校，为大家拍摄一期学五食堂的美食视频。

怀憧憬以前行

我第一次来中国是在 2006 年，北京奥运会之前。这么多年来，我见证了中国的飞速发展。每一次来到中国，我都能感受到新的变化。中国的发展速度之快，让我深感震撼。城市建设日新月异，科技发展突飞猛进，人们的生活水平不断提高。我看到中国在各个领域取得成就，这让我对中国充满了敬意和钦佩。那些

北航国际学生运动队

曾经和我一起留学的同学大多回到韩国发展，但我会一直留在中国，因为我深知中国这片土地充满了无限的可能。对于未来，我早已有了明确的规划和目标，我坚定地选择在这里继续发展自己的事业。

我渴望成为中韩人民交流的桥梁，让更多的中国人可以通过我了解韩国，也让更多的韩国人可以通过我了解中国。我希望"韩国大猪哥"这个名字能成为中韩友谊的代名词，用我的实际行动和影响力，加强两国人民之间的相互理解，增进友谊。为了实现这个目标，我计划不断提升自己的自媒体影响力，制作更多优质的内容，吸引更多的粉丝。我还打算与更多的品牌和机构合作，开展一些有意义的活动，促进中韩文化交流。此外，我也希望能够在未来有机会参与一些公益项目，为社会做出自己的贡献。

我目前所拥有的一切离不开朋友的帮助和支持。毕业后，我们虽然走上了不同的道路，但仍然保持着联系，互相支持和鼓励。我的中国朋友也为我的自媒体事业提供了很多帮助。他们会给我提供一些创意和建议，帮助我拍摄视频，还会在我遇到困难时给予我鼓励。我非常感激我的朋友们，没有他们的帮助，我不可能取得今天的成绩。

愿你们不负韶华

我非常想对在中国读书的学弟学妹们说：珍惜你们在北航的每时每刻。北航是一所优秀的学府，这里有丰富的学术资源和优秀的老师，你们要充分利用这些资源，努力学习，不断提升自己的能力。不要害怕走出自己的舒适圈，多与中国的同学们交流互动。他们不仅拥有深厚的学术素养，更怀揣着善良和热情。与他们相处，你们将拓宽自己的视野，领略到不同文化的魅力。记住，每一次交流都是一次宝贵的学习机会，都将为你们的人生增添一抹独特的色彩。勇敢地迈出第一步，与中国的同学们共同成长、共同进步吧！

后记：金大洙，这位毕业不满 10 年的校友，在异国的土地上奋斗与成长，挥洒青春激情，书写精彩华章。他的经历为学弟学妹们提供了宝贵的经验和启示，告诉他们要珍惜身边人、身边事，珍视每一个机会，要以确定的实力，迎接不确定的未来。

Beihang University Aspirations

I have been deeply fascinated by airplanes and other aircraft since a very young age. When my father moved to Beijing for a job transfer, I came with him and thereby got the chance to experience China's education system. During this process, I was initially captivated by Beihang University's renowned reputation in the aerospace sector. As I delved deeper, I was further impressed by its advanced teaching facilities, exceptional faculty, and rich academic resources, which collectively provide an outstanding environment for students' development. Encouraged by these factors, I chose Beihang University without hesitation and embarked on my challenging yet rewarding academic journey.

When I first arrived in China, all the Chinese words I knew were simple greetings like "Hello" and "Thank you." However, I knew that language was the key to my integration into a new environment, so I decided to overcome the language barrier. I started learning Chinese at Beijing Normal University, where systematic courses and conversations with teachers and classmates helped me improve quickly. Soon, I achieved the required Chinese proficiency for international students applying to Beihang University's undergraduate programs.

However, it was still a massive challenge for me to adapt to the all-Chinese teaching environment. Throughout my freshman year, the language barrier followed me everywhere I went. I found it was too hard to understand what teachers taught in class. To overcome this, I put in an immense amount of effort. After class, I would go through my books word by word, checking each word in the dictionary, marking pronunciations and translations, and reviewing them repeatedly. In addition, I often turned to my Chinese classmates for help. Their enthusiasm, coupled with their patience in answering my questions, helped me gradually adapt to the learning environment. I would chat with my Chinese friends and participate in all kinds of activities. By actively using Chinese in these situations, my language ability improved a lot. In my second year, I was finally able to understand the professional lectures, felt as if dark clouds had been lifted from my head. That was really a tough time, but it was my persistence and effort that enabled me to take a solid step forward on my academic journey.

My favorite course was Aircraft Structural Design. This course equipped me with in-depth knowledge of aircraft structural principles and design methodologies. Furthermore, through practical case studies and project implementations, my innovative thinking and problem-solving skills were significantly enhanced. After the study of this course, I also had the opportunity to team up with Chinese classmates and participate in the aircraft model design competition, where we achieved excellent results. This valuable experience not only helped me consolidate my professional knowledge but also greatly deepened my friendships with my Chinese peers and fostered a strong sense of teamwork among us.

My time here brought even more than these benefits. Besides absorbing a wealth of knowledge and mastering professional skills, I also forged friendships with numerous close friends, among whom my Chinese friends held a particularly significant meaning for me. Their selfless support and assistance in both my studies and work become the most cherished part of my overseas study experience. I once participated in the campus singing competition, though I only made it to the semifinals. This experience allowed me to meet many Chinese friends. We rehearsed and performed together, creating lots of joyful memories. All these things offered me the opportunities to feel the vibrant and diverse campus culture of Beihang University and made my overseas study life more fulfilling and meaningful.

More importantly, I learned how to get along with people and work as a team. These experiences have made me more mature and confident. However, I do have some regrets. At the start of my time at Beihang University, I was confident that my admission grades were outstanding. Thus, I didn't put enough effort into study and missed many opportunities to improve my grades. The grades at the end of my freshman year served as a wake-up call, prompting me to work diligently to catch up and not let my youth slip away. If I could start all over again, I would study harder to meet the expectations of my dear teachers, my alma mater and myself.

When I attended the 2021 graduation ceremony, I posted on social media:" My student days, the best time of my life, have come to an end. Last year, due to the pandemic, we only had an online ceremony. Thanks to my alma mater for inviting the 2020 graduates to attend this year's ceremony. Being here today, standing on Beihang University's playground, fills me with immense joy and nostalgia for my student years. During my four undergraduate years, though I was an international student, the bond I shared with my Chinese classmates was profoundly deep. In my studies, they taught me so much about Chinese culture, broadening my horizons and deepening my understanding of China. In daily life, they provided me with immense help, enabling me to successfully complete my studies."

Now, although I have entered the workplace, I often recall the good times we shared. I want to say the following words to my classmates: "Congratulations to all graduates! I hope we can meet again someday." The reason I am still working in China today is the deep appreciation for the country that my university classmates instilled in me.

The International School means a lot for international students. The faculty at the International School left a lasting impression on me, especially Ms. Yan Zhang, the teaching assistant. She was strict in academic matters yet always warm and kind in her interactions with us. My counselor, Xu Liu, also offered me great support. And the teacher I found it hardest to forget was my graduation project advisor, Professor Jidong Wang, from the School of Aeronautics and Astronautics Engineering. We have maintained contact until this day. In 2020, my graduation thesis defense could only be completed online. During this process, Professor Wang provided me with immense guidance and support, serving as a beacon illuminating my path forward. He gave me professional suggestions and instruction, and cared about my personal life and future plans. I am truly grateful to Professor Wang, and I deem him an important life mentor who has a profound impact on my development.

Pleasant Surprise

I've always dreamed of starting my own business after graduation, but the pandemic impacted this plan. When I returned to China post-pandemic, a Chinese classmate interning at Douyin suggested that cyberspace had tremendous potential, and I might as well try to be a social media content creator. I didn't have any ideas or plans, but giving it a try wouldn't cost anything. So I started sharing my life, stories, and perspectives on social media, gradually gaining some followers. Social media creation allowed me to express my ideas and connect with more people. My first video, filmed in 2021, was about Xinjiang-style fried rice noodles. I didn't know how to edit or film well at that time, so I learned while working on it. To be honest, I didn't have high expectations, but the result was surprisingly good.

When I first started filming in public, passersby would always curiously approach and ask what I was doing, which made me feel shy and unnatural, unsure of what to say when facing the camera. And I'd encounter staff members inquiring or stopping me. There were times when I traveled far to explore a specific restaurant, only to be turned away, forcing me to find alternative content on the spot. Despite encountering numerous difficulties, I've overcome them all. Now, even when fans show upon my camera to say hello, I can handle it naturally, and I'm more comfortable with editing and management. A video I filmed in Yanbian, titled *Korean Guy's First Experience in Yanbian* gained millions of views, introducing me to a larger audience. This prompted me to pursue content creation as a career, embarking on a journey full of challenges. I believe that if I persist, I will achieve my dreams.

As a food vlogger, if I could film a food video about Beihang University, I would definitely choose the newly-built No. 5 Cafeteria at the Xueyuan Road campus. It has a wide variety of delicious dishes, and the spacious, bright dining area creates a joyful atmosphere. I look forward to filming a food video for my followers and introducing my favorite cafeteria to them.

Forge Ahead with Nostalgia

My first visit to China was before the Beijing Olympics, back in 2006. Over these past years, I've witnessed China's rapid development. On each visit, I discovered new things that evidenced the astounding speed of China's progress. Urban development is progressing at a rapid pace, and scientific and technological advancements are making leaps and bounds, enhancing people's living standards. I've seen achievements across many fields, instilling deep respect and admiration for China. Most of my classmates have returned to the Republic of Korea, but I will continue my journey in China with clear plans and goals for the future. I am fully aware of the unlimited possibilities here, so I am determined to develop my career in this promising land.

I aspire to become a bridge for exchanges between China and the Republic of Korea, allowing more Chinese to learn about the Republic of Korea, and vice versa. I hope "Korean Brother DAZHU" becomes synonymous with the friendship of China and the Republic of Korea, promoting mutual understanding and building strong bonds. To achieve this, I need to create more high-quality videos to attract more followers, constantly enhancing my influence in this area. I also hope to collaborate with more brands and institutions on meaningful activities to promote cultural exchange between China and the Republic of Korea. In addition, I wish to have the opportunity to participate in philanthropic projects in the future to do my bit for society.

The support and help of my friends are indispensable for my achievements today. After graduation, although we each embarked on different paths, we have remained in touch, supporting and encouraging each other. For instance, they've offered me creative ideas and suggestions, assisted me in shooting videos, and given me encouragement and support whenever I encountered difficulties. I won't be who I am today without their help.

Embrace Your Youth

To the junior students studying in China, I'd like to say: Cherish every moment here. It's an outstanding university with abundant academic resources and excellent faculty, so make the most of these to enhance your abilities. Don't be afraid to get out of your comfort zone and communicate more with Chinese classmates. They possess rich academic knowledge and kindness. Interacting with them will expand your worldview and immerse you in different cultures. Remember, every exchange with them is a valuable learning opportunity that will add a unique color to your life. Take the first step bravely and grow together with your Chinese classmates!

Epilogue: Within ten years of graduating, Kim Daesu has been striving and growing on this foreign soil, writing the magnificent chapters of his life. His experiences serve as an inspiration to his juniors: cherish the people and events around you, and seize every opportunity. The future is uncertain, but we can continuously enhance our abilities to face it.

The Studying Story of
"Tie Bao"

03

"铁宝"求学记

北京航空航天大学

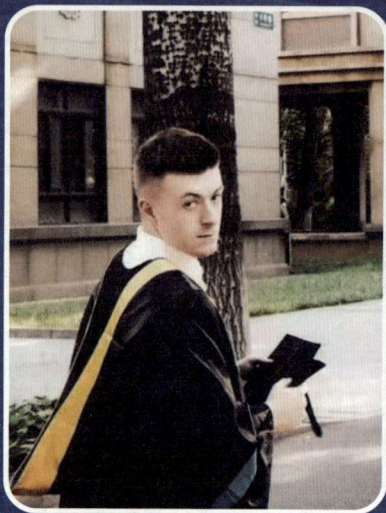

张浩成

    张浩成（Thibaud Soulier），法国校友，2014 年 9 月至 2015 年 7 月在北航汉语培训中心进行汉语研修，2015 年 9 月至 2019 年 7 月就读于北航经济管理学院国际经济与贸易专业，后前往北京大学攻读硕士学位。毕业后曾任职于西湖大学教学事务部，现居上海，任职于法国赛诺菲公司。

    Haocheng Zhang (or Thibaud Soulier in French), an alumnus from France, studied Chinese at Chinese Language Teaching Center of Beihang University from September 2014 to July 2015. He then pursued a Bachelor's degree in International Economics and Trade at the School of Economics and Management of Beihang University from September 2015 to July 2019, before furthering his studies for a Master's degree at Peking University. After graduation, he worked at the Academic Affairs Office of Westlake University. He is currently employed by Sanofi, a French multinational pharmaceutical company, and resides in Shanghai.

　　我叫张浩成，法文名字是 Thibaud Soulier，是北航 2019 届本科毕业生，目前在赛诺菲公司从事人力资源工作。在公司里，大家都喜欢管我叫"铁宝"，一方面是因为"铁宝"的谐音和我的法文名字比较相似，另一方面是因为我长得健壮如铁。非常荣幸能和大家分享我与中国的渊源，以及我在北航的学习和生活经历。作为比大家多走了几步路的学长，我希望能分享一些亲身经验，帮助各位更好地面对日后的学习生活。

初识中国

　　我与中国的缘分要追溯到 2003 年。当时，我在法国专注于练习竞技体操。与众多崇拜法国足球明星的人不同，我的偶像是中国体操运动员李小双。李小双是第一个成功完成"团身后空翻三周"的中国选手，他以出色的技艺成为当时中国体操的代表性人物。他在 1992 年巴塞罗那奥运会上出色完成动作的那一场比赛我至少看了上百遍，记得当时教练也经常让我们去看他的动作解析。因为体操，我对中国产生了最初的好感。

　　可惜的是，由于多种原因，我在初中时不得不放弃体操。但我从未停止对体操的热爱，现在我还常常会去国际赛场上观赛，也算是用另一种方式让这个爱好"复活"了。在 2024 年杭州举行的全国体操锦标赛上，很巧，

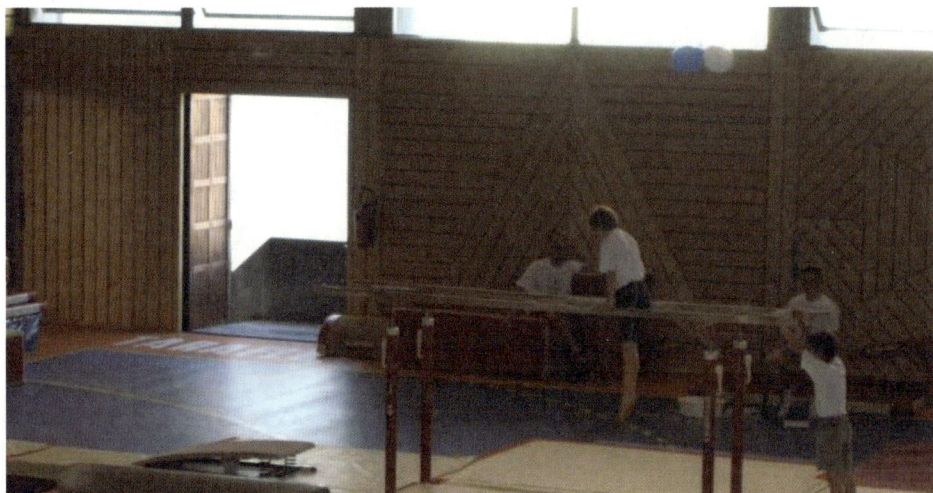

练习竞技体操

我碰到了李小双——我心中敬仰的小双哥。当我跟他谈及我小时候在房间挂满他的照片时，他感动万分。

失去"体操"这个挚爱后，我感觉自己每天都像个机器人，机械地应付生活中的各种事务，内心缺乏明确的方向和目标，我也不再是家庭聚会中的"奇迹男孩"。我深陷在这种状态中，直到 2010 年，我偶然看了一部名为《功夫梦》的电影。电影的背景设定在北京，影片中展现的城市氛围深深吸引了我，这种吸引力很难用语言来描述，让我觉得北京的生活充满了无限的可能性。影片中的场景让我感受到了一种陌生而又熟悉的归属感，也点燃了我心中对中国的探索欲。

那时，我正就读高一，还没确定高中毕业后的选择。内心的迷茫促使我认真思考未来的发展方向。这部电影让我意识到，或许我可以在中国探索更多的可能性，寻找属于我的生活路径。于是，我决定开始寻找各种汉语培训项目，希望能够更深入地了解中国的语言和文化。

北航之旅

在各大学的汉语培训项目中，我选择了北航的，从此与北航结下了很深的缘分。回想起刚到北航的第一年，我全身心投入学习，尽管过程辛苦，但我觉得自己真正做到了"知行合一"。每天背单词、背课文、背语法结构，虽然艰难，但最终的回报让我获得了巨大的成就感。

我的学习过程并不顺利。原本以为在这样一个语言环境中我会自然而然地掌握汉语，但实际情况却让我感到沮丧。刚开始的几个月，我对自己的语言水平很不满意，内心产生了较大的落差。我曾多次与国际学院的老师探讨这个问题，甚至一度申请住进中国学生的宿舍，希望通过更深入的交流提高自己的汉语水平。

好在我的性格比较执着，或许这也是我觉得"铁宝"这个昵称比较适合自己的原因，面对困难时我反而更加严格要求自己，决心要克服这一切。我觉得自己是一个非常"偏科"的人，不光能力上，性格上也是，对于自己想做的事情，总是拿出所有狠劲儿去奋斗，但是如果对某件事情不是那么想做，就会变得有点随波逐流。

给小学生讲法国文化

于是，为了克服语言上遇到的困难，我开始制订各种"反人类"的学习计划。例如，每天背几页《新华字典》，生活中完全用汉语，并且随时记录和背诵遇到的生词。现在回想当时的自己还真有点励志。虽然学习方法在初期有些生硬，但这种坚持为我的本科学习奠定了坚实的基础。有一次，我走在五道口的大街上，突然发现自己能够理解所有路标和店名的意思了。这种进步让我豁然开朗，心中充满了信心，也让我进入了一个良性循环，学习效果越来越显著。

汉语培训项目结束后，我面临两种选择：要么回到法国读大学，要么继续留在北航读本科。我心中始终放不下对中国的探索与热爱，经过深思熟虑，我决定抓住申请的最后期限，留在北航，开启四年的本科学习之旅。我清晰地记得国际学院的朱老师当时对我说的话，"你这个人性格真是干脆"，这让我第一次深刻理解了"干脆"这个词的真正含义。

然而，我的本科生活并非一帆风顺。第一年，我的数学基础较弱，经历了不少困难，但凭借不服输的性格，我坚持到底，最终克服了这一难关。

工作中的"铁宝"（左一）

我认为，在北航的这段时间是我人生的一个关键转折点。正是在北航的学习经历，为我创造了更多的机会。

我现在工作的公司是法国著名企业，能够进入这样的公司，意味着我在中国所有的努力与拼搏得到了认可。在职场中，汉语流利的外国人虽然不少，但像我这样拥有独特经历的人却属于"稀有动物"。这种经历使我在职场中拥有了一定的优势。身处在华的法国企业，面对法国和中国的同事，我在两种语言中切换自如，这使我的工作得心应手。当我与同事分享自己的经历时，人们总是对我刮目相看，称赞我追逐自己心之所向的勇气和决心。能够在这样一个多元化的环境中工作，我感到无比自豪。

饮水而思源

北航不仅是我开启学术生涯的重要一站，更是我在中国探险之旅的起点。我对这个校园充满感情，我还记得每天上学路上的小吃、合一楼的烧鸭饭，以及超市的零食。尽管我在北航的朋友们现在已经分散在世界各地，但我仍然与他们保持联系。北航非常适合法国学生来学习，因为这里有很多中法交流的机会，听说杭州新开设了中法航空学院，在新的教学园区里应该有更好的国际氛围。

北航的硬件设施非常齐全，学习氛围浓厚，各种课外活动和有趣的小彩蛋也让我的校园生活丰富多彩。我曾在中国的其他地方待过，但没有任何一个地方能像北航一样让我感受到归属感。走在校园里，即使认识的同学都已毕业，但这里的一切仍让我感到亲切，仿佛回到了"起点"，重新充电。知春路一带也始终让我有这种熟悉感，回到此处，仿佛一个游戏通关后又回到了第一关，令人欣慰的熟悉感油然而生。

在北航的这段经历让我不仅提升了学业水平，也锻炼了能力。无论是语言学习、社交能力，还是职场经验，这些都将对我的未来发展起到重要的推动作用。回望选择赴华留学、来到北航的决定，我深感庆幸。如果有机会对当年的自己说一句话，我会说："谢谢你，选择了这条路。"在未来的日子里，我希望能继续探索更多的机会，将自己的经验和能力用于更广泛的领域。我相信，在中国的这段经历将成为我人生旅途中的重要部分，激励我不断追求卓越，开创美好的未来。

对国际学生的建议

如果让我给国际学生提一个建议，那就是：给我学，给我学，给我狠狠地学。在学习的过程中，一定要挖掘自己的闪光点，充分利用你们在中国的机会，深入了解中华文化，并学好汉语。我强烈建议大家毕业后努力留在中国就业。当前，中国在许多领域，尤其是与工科相关的领域，已经走在了全球前沿。在这个高速发展的商业环境中，虽然会面临挑战，但个人成长也会非常迅速。如果能说一口流利的汉语，那简直是"王炸"。最重要的是，要以正确、严肃的态度完成学业，在中国完成全日制高等教育的本科四年里，不能简单地玩乐或旅行，这是获得重要学历的机会。英语中有句话——"You are what you do"，要像对待自己的前途一样认真对待学习，你如今的每一步都在为未来铺路。

　　我也希望给正在北航就读的各位喊一声"加油"。你们正处于人生中最重要的学习阶段，面对无数的机会与挑战，希望你们珍惜时光，充分利用学校的资源，努力提升自己的能力。学习固然重要，但也要积极参与课外活动，结交不同背景的朋友，丰富自己的人生阅历。记住，每一步努力都将为你们的未来打下坚实的基础。加油，期待你们在校内外创造辉煌成就！

My name is Haocheng Zhang, or Thibaud Soulier in French. I graduated from Beihang University in 2019 and currently work in human resources at Sanofi in Shanghai. My colleagues always call me "Tie Bao", because it sounds similar to my French name, and indeed, I am strong and sturdy like iron. It is a great honor to be here to share with you my connection with China, as well as my study and life experiences at Beihang University. As an alumnus, I hope I can share some of my experiences with you all, to help you better navigate the challenges of your future studies and life.

Discover China

My connection with China dates back to 2003. During that time, all my attention was paid to practicing gymnastics in France. Different from the fans of French football stars, my idol was the Chinese gymnast Xiaoshuang Li. He was definitely a representative of Chinese gymnastics then, for he was the first Chinese athlete to successfully complete the "triple back somersault on floor". I watched that competition where he executed his routine brilliantly at the 1992 Barcelona Olympics repeatedly at least a hundred times, and my coach often asked us to watch the analysis of his movements. Because of gymnastics, I developed an initial fondness for China.

Unfortunately, I had to quit gymnastics in middle school due to various reasons. But I never stop my love for gymnastics. Even now I always go to watch national championship matches. It is kind of revitalizing my hobby in another way. Fortunately, at the national gymnastics championship held in Hangzhou in 2024, I met Xiaoshuang Li, who by then had become my "Xiaoshuang brother". He was deeply moved that I filled my room with his photos when I was just a kid.

After quitting gymnastics, the sport I devoted to, I felt like I was living as a robot without any clear motivation and goals, just mechanically finishing routine tasks in daily life. I had been immersed in this emotional state until 2010, when I watched a movie called *The Karate Kid* by chance, and its setting is in Beijing.

It was the city's atmosphere portrayed in this movie that deeply attracted me. It is hard to describe this attraction in words, but it made me feel that life in China might be filled with infinite possibilities. The scenes in the movie evoked a sense of belonging that was both strange and familiar, igniting my desire to explore China within me.

At that time, I was in my first year of high school and unsure of my choices after graduation. The confusion in my heart drove me to seriously reflect upon the direction of my future. This movie let me realize that perhaps I could explore more possibilities in China and find my own path in life. Thus, I decided to start looking for various Chinese training programs, hoping to gain a deeper understanding of the Chinese and culture.

Journey at Beihang University

Among the various Chinese training programs offered by different universities, I chose Beihang University's, which has since become a significant part of my journey. Looking back on my first year here, I devoted myself to studying. Although the process was arduous, I felt that I truly achieved "the unity of knowledge and action". Every day, I memorized vocabulary, texts, and even grammatical structures. It was challenging, but the sense of accomplishment I gained in the end was incredibly fulfilling.

My initial learning process was not that smooth. I had assumed that being in such a language-rich environment would naturally help me master Chinese, but the reality left me feeling frustrated. For the first few months, I was dissatisfied with my language skills, which created a significant gap between my expectations and reality. I often discussed this issue with my teachers at the International School and even applied to live in a dormitory with Chinese students, hoping that deeper immersion would improve my Chinese skills.

Fortunately, my personality is rather "stubborn", perhaps that is why I think the nickname "Tie Bao" suits me well. When faced with challenges, I tend to push myself even harder and am determined to overcome any obstacles. I am someone who is quite "imbalanced"—both in abilities and personality. If I am passionate about something, I will pour all my effort into it, but if I am not deeply interested, I tend to go with the flow.

To tackle my language difficulties, I devised a series of what I now call "inhuman" study plans. For example, I would memorize several pages of the Xinhua Dictionary every day, live a life fully immersed in Chinese, and constantly note down and recite new words I encountered. Looking back, I find my past self quite inspiring. My methods may be somewhat rigid initially, but this persistence laid a solid foundation for my undergraduate studies. I vividly remember the moment when I was walking down the streets of Wudaokou and suddenly found that I could understand all the street signs and store names. This progress was a revelation, filling me with confidence and propelling me into a virtuous cycle. Leading to exponential improvements in my learning outcomes.

After finishing my language studies, I faced two choices: return to France to attend university or stay at Beihang University for my undergraduate studies. My passion for exploring and loving China made the decision clear. After careful consideration, I submitted my application right before the deadline. I decided to seize the opportunity to stay at Beihang University and embark on a four-year undergraduate journey. I still remember what Teacher Zhu from the International School said to me clearly: "You are such a decisive person." That was the first time I deeply understood the meaning of the Chinese word "gan cui" (decisive).

My undergraduate life, however, was not without its challenges. During my first year, my weak math skills caused significant difficulties. Yet, driven by my unwillingness to give up, I persevered and ultimately overcame this hurdle. I believe my time at Beihang University was a pivotal turning point in my life. It was this experience that created more opportunities for me.

Today, I work at one of France's top companies. Being able to join such a prestigious firm is a recognition of all my efforts and hard work in China. In the workplace, there are many foreigners fluent in Chinese, though individuals with unique experiences like mine are rare. This background has given me a certain advantage in my career. Working in a French company in China, I effortlessly navigate between French and Chinese colleagues, switching between the two languages with ease. When I share my experiences with others, they are often impressed by my courage and determination to pursue what I truly want. Working in such a multicultural environment fills me with immense pride.

Remember the Roots

Beihang University is not only a part of my academic journey but also the starting point of my adventure in China. I have a deep love for this campus. I still remember the food stalls I passed every day on my way to class, the Roast Duck rice at He Yi Lou (a canteen at Beihang University), and the snacks from the campus supermarket. The friends I met are living in different places all around the world, yet we still stay in touch. Beihang University is especially well-suited for French students, as there are many opportunities for Sino-French exchanges. I've heard that a new Zhongfa Aviation Institute has recently opened in Hangzhou, and I believe the new campus will offer an even better cultural atmosphere.

Beihang University's facilities are top-notch, and the academic environment is rich. The various extracurricular activities and interesting hidden gems made my campus life vibrant and fulfilling. Although I've lived in other parts of China, no place has given me the same sense of belonging as Beihang University. Walking through the campus, even though many of my classmates have graduated, everything still felt familiar. It's as if I've returned to the starting point, ready to recharge. Zhichun Road also evokes this comforting familiarity, like revisiting the first level of a game after completing it, filling me with a reassuring sense of nostalgia.

Through my experiences at Beihang University, I not only improved academically but also developed my life skills. Whether it was language learning, social abilities, or professional experience, they have all played a significant role in shaping my future. Reflecting on my decision to study abroad in China and attend Beihang University, I feel incredibly fortunate. If I could say one thing to my younger self, it would be: "Thank you for choosing this path." Looking ahead, I hope to continue exploring new opportunities and applying my experiences and skills to broader fields. I believe that my time in China will remain a crucial part of my life's journey, inspiring me to pursue excellence and build a brighter future.

Advice for International Students

If I were to give one piece of advice to international students, it would be this: Study, study, and study hard! During your studies, make sure to discover your unique strengths and make the most of your time in China. Dive deep into understanding Chinese culture, society, and language. I strongly encourage you to strive to stay in China for work after graduation. Nowadays, China is taking the lead in many fields, especially engineering and technology. In this rapidly evolving business environment, while challenges are inevitable, personal growth is equally fast-paced. If you can speak fluent Chinese, it's like having a "trump card" in your hands. Most importantly, complete your studies with the right mindset and a serious attitude. Studying full-time in China for four years is not just about having fun or traveling. It's a valuable opportunity to earn a significant degree. As the saying goes, "You are what you do." Treat your undergraduate studies with the same seriousness as your future. Every step you take today is paving the way for your future.

To all the current students at Beihang University, I want to cheer you on. You are at one of the most critical stages of your academic journey, facing countless opportunities and challenges. I hope you cherish your time, make full use of university's resources, and strive to enhance your skills. While studying is important, don't forget to actively participate in extracurricular activities, connect with friends from diverse backgrounds, and enrich your life experiences. Remember, every effort you put in now will lay a solid foundation for your future. Best of luck, and I look forward to seeing you achieve greatness both on and off campus!

My Zambian Heritage
and Innovation Ability
Blend Here

04

我的赞比亚血脉与创新能力
在此交融

田仁治

　　从赞比亚到中国，田仁治（Stanley Musonda）的求学和创业之路跨越了文化与技术的边界。在北航求学期间，他经历了从语言挑战到科研磨砺的过程。北航提供的学术资源和独特的跨文化环境，让他收获了丰富的专业知识，更激发了他成为企业家的梦想。毕业后，他做出了留在中国创业的决定。如今，他的公司已迈向国际市场，服务多个国家和地区。这段从留学到创业的旅程，不仅让他实现了自我价值，更让他深感责任重大，他期望为中非之间的经济合作贡献自己的力量。

　　From Zambia to China, Stanley Musonda's journey of education and enterpreneurship has transcended cultural and technological boundaries. During his time at Beihang University, he went through a process from language challenges to scientific research trials. The academic resources and unique cross-cultural environment provided by Beihang University enabled him to gain rich professional knowledge and, more importantly, inspired his dream of becoming an entrepreneur. After graduation, he decided to stay in China to start his own business. Today, his company has entered the international market, serving multiple countries and regions. This journey from studying abroad to starting a business has not only allowed him to realize his self-worth but also made him deeply aware of his responsibility to contribute to the economic cooperation between China and Africa.

扫码观看
采访视频

我是 Stanley Musonda，来自赞比亚，中文名字是田仁治。我就读的本科院校是西北工业大学。本科毕业以后，我先是回到了赞比亚民航局做无人机工程师，后来又在中国—赞比亚职业技术学院任教，主要负责指导矿工操作数控机床等机械设备，也会给学生上编程课。因为想继续深造，所以我在 2019 年来到北航攻读硕士学位。在这所世界一流学府的学习经历对我的人生产生了非常大的影响，这里多元的文化环境也促使我飞速成长，我开始重新思考我的职业道路，并最终决定去创业。

语言障碍：最初的难关

2019 年是我人生中的一个转折点，这一年我在北航学习了一整年的汉语。汉语非我母语，学汉语对我来说无疑是一大难关。陌生的汉字以及两种语言在结构上的巨大差异都让我无所适从，但同时我非常清楚，学好汉语是我在中国好好生活、好好学习的前提。

经过不懈努力，我逐渐熟悉了汉语的发音和语法，甚至还能与老师、同学进行基本的对话。初步掌握汉语让我能更好地融入学术环境，也让我对中华文化有了更深刻的理解，这为我未来的学习和创业打下了基础。学习汉语虽难，这段经历却是无价之宝。

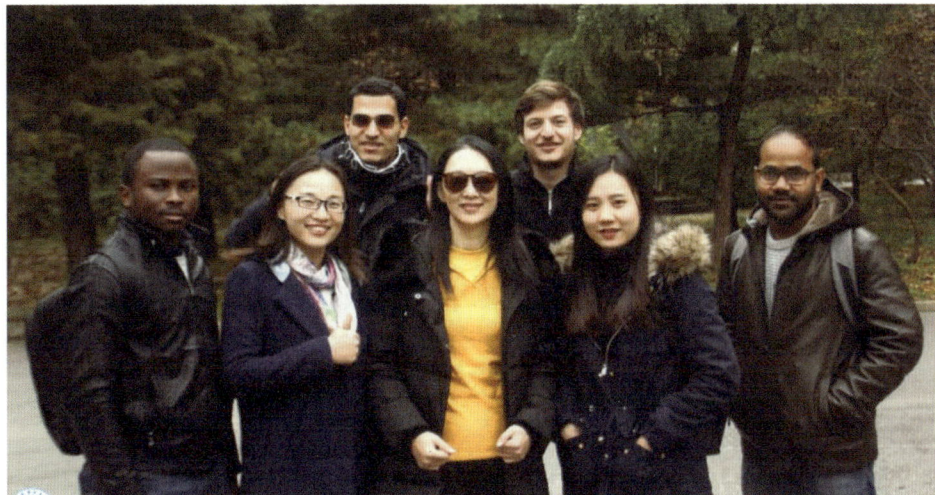

田仁治（左一）所在北航国际学院汉语培训班合照

求学经历

　　2020 年，我正式成为北航的研究生，主修机械制造与自动化。我是在深思熟虑后才选择的这个专业，考虑到我以往的工作经历和赞比亚的发展需求，我认为这个专业是我的不二之选。并且我本身是一名科技爱好者，对这一领域的前沿技术非常感兴趣。选择在北航学

汉语课上学写毛笔字

习这个专业，是因为北航在航空航天和机械工程领域享有极高的全球声誉。

　　研究生的课程安排很紧张，尤其是在第一学年，我们有很多技术课程，包括控制系统、计算机辅助设计（CAD）/ 计算机辅助制造（CAM）技术等，这些课程拓宽了我的知识面，提高了我的学习能力，但也真的让我"压力山大"。我告诉自己这些难关都是进步的机会，事实也的确如此。在攻克这些难关的过程中，我的时间管理、资源利用和团队协作能力都得到了锻炼，我顺利地完成了所有的课程作业。

　　研二的时候，我就把学习重心放在了我的研究项目上。我研究的是一个关于胶囊内窥镜机器的多元项目，涉及用磁力控制胶囊，还要开发定位程序。我不仅要做实验、分析数据，还要写一篇全面的研究论文。反复实验过程中的各种不确定性及挫折让我倍感压力，但我还是坚持了下来，在过程中不断学习，最终成功完成了论文并顺利毕业。这段学术旅程就是这样，在困难和障碍中不断提升我的能力和韧性，让我能够更好地迎接未来在职业生涯中的挑战。

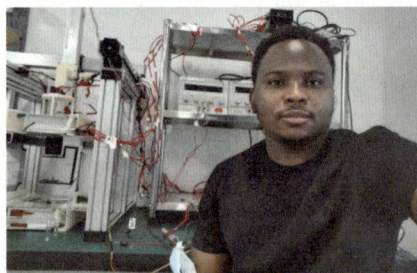

在实验室做实验

在北航的难忘时刻

　　回顾我在北航的三年时光，有许多值得铭记的时刻。最让我难忘的是

2020 年年初疫情暴发的时候，当时全世界的人们都很不安，没有人知道接下来会发生什么，而我孤身一人在外求学，没办法与家人团聚，心里非常难受。

那个时期确实非常难熬，但是各位老师对我们国际学生的关怀和帮助让我非常感动。我清晰地记得，为了解决我们这些无法回家的国际学生的需求，刘娜院长在疫情期间一直住在学校里面。除了解决生活上的问题，她还特别关心我们的心理状态。她的做法让我体会到北航浓浓的人情味，也让我下定决心留在中国继续学习和生活。

也是在这段时间，我想要创业的念头越来越强烈，因为当时许多企业无法来华，他们联系上我，让我帮忙处理许多事。这个过程让我看到了未来职业发展的另一种可能，埋下了我创业的种子。

创业的灵感与机遇

毕业后，我做出了一个重大的决定——我要留在中国创业！做这个决定不是一时冲动，在北航的求学经历开阔了我的眼界，也让我个人飞速成长，我认为留在这片土地上创业是正确的选择。全球联系日益紧密，我意识到自己作为一名与中国联系紧密且具备专业知识的非洲青年，可以成为沟通中国与赞比亚，甚至与整个非洲先进技术需求的桥梁。

像我前面所说的那样，许多国际企业和个人无法进入中国，这意外地暴露出市场的空白，也显现出了我身份的特殊性。此外，我的导师冯林教授创办公司的成功案例，也极大地鼓舞着我。他的成功让我坚信，只要有决心、不放弃，我也一定能在中国实现自己的创业梦想。

市场机会、个人背景和技术知识都已具备，中国当时的环境也利好，可以说是天时、地利、人和，所以我决心要实现从学生到企业家的转变，利用我的知识和跨文化背景，在中国这个充满活力的商业环境中创造价值。

田仁治（左）与导师冯林教授合影

从学生到CEO：我的创业之旅

2023年，我迈出了创业的第一步。起初，我们从事一般贸易，以满足不同客户的需求。到2024年，我们的业务集中在两个领域：提供汽车车身维修设备和工具，以及为制造业、矿山和车间提供空气净化设备。作为首席执行官（CEO），我主要负责日常运营，同时也积极寻求市场拓展机会。现在我们的业务已触及国际市场，产品销往俄罗斯、英国、加拿大及非洲多国。

公司内景

创业之路布满荆棘。作为一家初创公司，我们需要不断提升自身能力，才能满足国际市场日益变化的需求。而搞清楚中国复杂的法律条文和贸易法规，对我们来说是一项艰巨的挑战。好在我得到了北航校友们的支持，有些校友成了我们的业务伙伴，有些在法律和财会方面提供专业支持，这让我对在中国创办一个成

田仁治在办公室

功的企业更有信心。尽管创业之路困难重重，但我在北航建立的人际网络和学习的技能，使我在应对国际贸易的复杂问题以及促进公司发展方面游刃有余。

北航影响力与中国创新力

在北航的求学经历是我个人履历中相当光彩的一笔，北航的背书让我

田仁治（左二）和北航同学们

在国际市场中更具竞争力。由于学校的全球知名度高，每次参加商业活动时，客户得知我毕业于北航后，都会对我青睐有加，这让我获得了很多宝贵的机会。北航的知名度也是我公司的信誉背书，在建立跨国业务的过程中发挥着重要作用，许多原本紧闭的大门因此向我敞开。

此外，中国出色的科技创新能力是我取得创业成功的基石。中国在制造和自动化领域的迅猛发展让我们能够为客户提供高质量产品和服务。与中国的供应商和技术专家的合作也让我们在技术上不断取得突破。中国在全球创新领域的领先地位使我们拥有先进的技术和方法，并始终处于行业前沿。

总之，北航卓越的学术地位和中国的创新生态，不仅推动了我职业道路的发展，也推动了我的公司在全球市场上的成长与成功。

心声寄学子

对想来中国读书的年轻人，我想说：要拥抱挑战，因为它们是成长的机会。在北航，语言不通和文化差异并不是阻碍，而是机遇。克服这些以后，你会收获更坚韧的自己。以开放和积极的心态面对坎坷吧，你从中所学到的每个技能在未来都会发挥重要的作用。

田仁治（右一）参加 2023 年学生毕业典礼

　　学业固然要紧，但广交贤达同样重要。不管是在学习中还是职场上，人际关系都是宝贵的财富。在北航，我结识了许多伙伴，他们对我和我的职业发展给予支持，在我的创业之路上发挥了举足轻重的作用。要不断建立和拓展社交网络，抓住每个与同学、教授和校友互动的机会，这些关系会为你未来的成功打下基础。创业过程很难，国际业务的环境很复杂，但这些宝贵的人脉会为你提供机遇和帮助。

　　好奇心和求知欲是每个有抱负的企业家所必备的品质。技术的快速发展要求我们不断学习，紧跟行业内外的创新趋势，持续搜寻新信息和新视角。坚持终身学习会让你做出正确的商业决策，走在行业前沿，有能力识别并抓住新兴趋势。在中国留学期间要着力提升自己的专业技能，这对你未来的成功至关重要。

　　风险的存在的确让人胆寒，但想脱颖而出，就要敢于冒险。我选择留在中国创业，这看似一步险棋，但却可能为我带来非凡的成果。走出舒适区固然很难，甚至我们会觉得自己不堪一击，但我们要接受这种脆弱，因为人在脆弱的时刻成长得最快。有韧性才能应对创业过程中的起起伏伏，若把挫折视为学习的机会，那它便会使你的决心更坚定。利用好在中国学习和生活的每一分每一秒吧，这段经历会赋予你独特的视角和宝贵的经验。

为"一带一路"倡议做出贡献

中国的"一带一路"倡议在加强全球经济联系方面发挥了重要作用，我为自己能参与这一变革性进程而感到自豪。该倡议在基础设施发展、贸易便利化和外国投资方面的战略重点，让我对非洲的持续进步和繁荣满怀期望。

"一带一路"倡议让我获得了大量的资源和广泛的人脉，大大增强了我的公司在中国和全球舞台上的影响力。赞比亚是参与"一带一路"共建的重要非洲国家，也是中国持续的合作伙伴。这种友好关系为两国基础设施投资、技术转让和经济合作开辟了新的渠道。

我热切鼓励和支持其他非洲企业家积极参与"一带一路"共建，通过合作进入中国这个充满活力的市场。鉴于中国坚定地建立互利合作关系，并加大对非洲相关国家的投资力度，我认为"一带一路"倡议是推动经济进步的变革性平台，将为中国和非洲国家带来共同利益。通过这些重要的合作渠道，我们可以获得前所未有的机会，提高经济水平，促进可持续发展，推动建设一个更加互联、更加繁荣的世界。

田仁治（前排中间）参加国际合作论坛

展望中非合作的未来

未来，我将致力于进一步推动中非之间的合作。在中国的经历让我看到了跨文化交流的强大力量，以及它对个人和职业发展的深远影响。我公司的规模正在不断扩大，我期望能打开更多非洲国家的市场，使更多国家能够接触到中国的技术优势和专业知识，从而促成经济和技术进步的互利循环。

我坚信，将非洲巨大的市场潜力与中国在制造业和创新领域的优势相结合，一定会有利于中非建立具有影响力的合作伙伴关系。我的目标是建立长期的、互惠互利的合作关系，以应对非洲国家在关键行业，例如制造业、农业和基础设施中的特定需求和挑战。以我在中国积累的经验和实践经历为鉴，我希望能促进非洲国家的经济增长，同时帮助中国企业进入快速发展的非洲市场。

我渴望成为推动进步的强大催化剂。我的愿景是推动知识共享、技术转让和经济合作的良性循环，使非洲国家实现更高级别的自给自足和繁荣，同时为中国企业开拓新的发展领域。通过引入先进设备、尖端技术和创新商业模式，整合这两个充满活力的地区的优势资源，我坚信我们可以抓住前所未有的机遇，实现共同的繁荣和可持续发展。

结语

如果我能给年少的自己一些建议，我会说：坚持你所做的每个选择，正是每一次的错误和抉择让你成为今天的你。在北航的学习和创业之旅，于我而言是一段充满挑战和非凡机遇的变革之旅。从一名在陌生环境中语言不通只能慢慢摸索的国际学生，成长为如今在中国拥有自己公司的企业家，一路走来，重重磨炼铸就了我在逆境中成长和抓住战略机遇的能力。我终于在多元文化的环境中闯出了自己的一片天地。前路漫长而曲折，但我定会持续提升，为不断扩大的客户群提供高质量的服务，希望能以此为中非之间日益紧密的经济合作贡献自己的力量。

北航赋予我独特的机遇，中国蓬勃发展的商业环境给我发展的空间。在向前迈出的每一步中，我都在力求用自己的经验和专业知识，在我的祖国——赞比亚与这个非凡的国家——中国之间创建合作的契机。我要向北航致以最深的感谢，是它带我踏上了这段改变人生的旅程；也要向伟大的中国表达我衷心的感谢，感谢它为我敞开了我梦寐以求的机遇之门。未来是光明灿烂的，我渴望继续走在这条让人收获友谊、成长和共同成功的道路上。我也期盼能助力中非合作，让中非友谊代代传唱。

导师寄语

　　作为田仁治的指导老师，我为他在北航的学术旅程和创业之路上所取得的成就感到无比骄傲。他的故事不仅是个人奋斗的象征，也是中非友谊与合作的生动写照。勇气、智慧和坚持让他在多元文化的交融中能绽放光彩。希望他继续以开放的心态拥抱挑战，用才华和热情，架起中非交流的桥梁，为两国的友谊与合作贡献力量。

导师简介

　　冯林，北航"卓越百人计划"教授，博士生导师，北京市杰出青年，北京市科技新星。入选 2011 年日本机械工程师学会优秀年轻学者、2013 年日本学术振兴会（JSPS）学者、2020 年电气电子工程师学会（IEEE）国际微纳米机器人技术委员会理事。目前担任 *Bio-Design and Manufacturing*、*Cyborg and Bionic Systems* 和 *SmartBot* 期刊编委，中国微米纳米技术学会微纳机器人分会、微纳操作器与执行器分会理事。曾任 IEEE 国际机器人和自动化会议（ICRA）、智能机器人与系统国际会议（IROS）的编委、分会主席。在 *International Journal of Robotics Research*、*Small*、*Research*、*Advanced Health Material*、*Advanced Intelligent System*、*Lab on a chip* 等 SCI/EI 收录期刊发表论文 160 余篇，出版教材《微纳米机器人概论》及英文专著共 4 部，获得省部级等奖项 30 余项，申请专利 40 余项。

I'm Musonda Stanley, known in Chinese as Renzhi Tian, and I'm from Zambia. After completing my undergraduate degree at Northwestern Polytechnical University, I returned to Zambia. There, I worked as a drone engineer for the Zambia Civil Aviation Authority before joining the China-Zambia Vocational and Technical College. At college, I was mainly responsible for instructing miners in operating CNC machines and other mechanical equipment while also teaching programming to college students. My journey to Beihang University began in 2019, driven by aspirations to broaden my educational and professional horizons. I decided to pursue a master's degree at one of the world's premier institutions—Beihang University. My time at Beihang University was transformative, not only redirecting my career path but also nurturing my personal growth in a diverse, multicultural setting. I started to rethink my career path and it was this experience ultimately led me to embark on an entrepreneurial journey.

Language Barrier: The Initial Challenge

2019 was a turning point in my life as I embarked on a year-long Chinese program at Beihang University. As a non-native speaker, grappling with Chinese proved to be a formidable challenge. The stark differences in language structure and the unfamiliar characters initially left me feeling daunted. However, I recognized that mastering Chinese was crucial for my academic success and life in China.

Through persistent dedication, I gradually acclimated to Chinese pronunciation and grammar. Eventually, I reached a level where I could engage in basic conversations with my peers and instructors. This linguistic foundation not only facilitated my integration into the academic environment but also enhanced my appreciation of Chinese culture. This newfound language proficiency laid the groundwork for my future studies, and my entrepreneurial endeavors ultimately. This language journey, while demanding, proved to be an invaluable asset.

Educational Experience

In 2020, I officially commenced my master's program at Beihang University, specializing in Mechanical Manufacturing and Automation. This choice was deliberate and aligned with my previous work experience and my nation's developmental needs. As a technology enthusiast, I was naturally attracted to cutting-edge advancements in mechanical manufacturing. Beihang University's global reputation in aerospace and mechanical engineering further solidified my decision.

The rigor of graduate-level coursework was intense, particularly during the first year. The demanding schedule encompassed numerous technical subjects, including control systems, CAD/CAM Technology, and more. These courses pushed the boundaries of my knowledge and learning capacity, often placing me under considerable pressure. However, I viewed these challenges as opportunities for personal growth, honing my time management skills, resource utilization, and collaborative abilities. By the end of that year, I had successfully completed all the required coursework.

The second year of my master's program was dedicated to research. I undertook a multifaceted project on Capsule Endoscopy Machines, which involved controlling the capsule using magnetism and developing localization programming. This phase demanded not only conducting experiments and analyzing data but also writing a comprehensive research thesis. Despite often feeling overwhelmed by the uncertainties and setbacks of repeated experiments, my perseverance and commitment to continuous learning enabled me to complete my thesis and graduate successfully. This academic journey not only enhanced my technical expertise but also honed my resilience and problem-solving skills, preparing me for future career challenges.

Unforgettable Moments at Beihang University

Reflecting on my three years at Beihang University, numerous memorable moments stand out. However, the most impactful experience occurred in early

2020, during the outbreak of the COVID-19 pandemic. As the world was suddenly engulfed in anxiety and uncertainty, being an international student far from home and unable to reunite with my family was emotionally challenging.

Throughout this period, the care and support by staff and faculty extended to us were truly remarkable. I vividly recall Vice-Dean Na Liu staying on campus during the pandemic, ensuring that those of us who couldn't return home had everything we needed. She not only helped us with practical issues but also provided emotional support. Her dedication demonstrated the warmth of the Beihang University community and reinforced my decision to continue studying and living in China.

It was during this time that my conviction to pursue entrepreneurship grew. As many businesses could not come to China due to the pandemic, they began to call on me for help with various matters. This experience planted the seeds for my business endeavors.

The Inspiration and Opportunity to Become an Entrepreneur

Upon completing my studies, I made the pivotal decision to remain in China and embark on an entrepreneurial journey. This choice was not spontaneous but rather the culmination of gradual insights and personal growth throughout my academic years. In our increasingly global world, I recognized that my unique position as a young professional with ties to both China and Africa could serve as a bridge, connecting Chinese technological advancements with the evolving needs of Zambia and potentially the broader African market.

As I said before, the global pandemic unexpectedly highlighted a significant market gap, as many international businesses and individuals were unable to enter China. This situation revealed numerous opportunities that I was uniquely positioned to address. Furthermore, the guidance and example set by my supervisor, Professor Lin Feng, who had successfully established his own company, served as a powerful source of inspiration. His accomplishments reinforced my belief that with determination and resilience, I also could realize my entrepreneurial ambitions in China.

This combination of market opportunity, personal background, technical knowledge, and China's environment solidified my resolve to transition from student to entrepreneur, leveraging my education and cross-cultural experiences to create value in this dynamic business environment.

From Student to CEO: My Entrepreneurial Journey

In 2023, I took the significant step of establishing my own company. Initially, we engaged in general trading to meet diverse client needs. By 2024, we have honed our focus to two primary areas: supplying auto body repair equipment and tools, and providing air purification equipment for manufacturing sectors, mines, and workshops. As the CEO, I oversee daily operations while actively pursuing market expansion opportunities. Our business has achieved international reach, with our products now being sold across several countries, including Russia, the UK, Canada, and various African nations.

The journey of entrepreneurship has presented numerous challenges. As a startup, we face the constant need to enhance our capabilities to meet the evolving demands of the international market. Navigating the complex landscape of legal and trade regulations in China has been a particularly significant hurdle. However, the network I cultivated during my time at Beihang University has proven invaluable. Friends and alumni have offered crucial support—some have become business partners, while others have provided essential legal and accounting guidance. This network has bolstered my confidence in building a successful enterprise in China. Despite the challenges, the support system and skills I developed at Beihang University have been crucial in navigating the complexities of international business and fostering the growth of my company.

Beihang University's Influence and China's Innovation Capacity

Beihang University has left an indelible mark on both my academic and professional journey. The university's global reputation has proven to be a significant asset for my business endeavors. Clients often express heightened admiration and trust upon learning about my Beihang University background, which has translated into valuable opportunities and a competitive edge in the international market. The prestige associated with Beihang University has not only bolstered my company credibility but has also opened doors that might otherwise have remained closed. This institutional backing has been instrumental in establishing cross-border business.

Moreover, China's remarkable capacity for technological innovation has been a cornerstone of my business success. The country's rapid advancements in manufacturing and automation have enabled us to offer cutting-edge, high-quality products and services to our clients. Our collaborations with Chinese suppliers and technical experts have catalyzed significant progress in our technological development. China's global leadership in innovation and entrepreneurship has created a powerful foundation for my business. It has allowed us to leverage state-of-the-art technologies and methodologies, ensuring that we remain at the forefront of our industry.

In essence, the combination of Beihang University's academic excellence and China's innovative ecosystem has not only shaped my professional trajectory but also continues to drive the growth and success of my enterprise in the global marketplace.

Heartfelt Voices to International Students

For young people planning to study in China, I would say: Embrace challenges, as they are growth opportunities. The language barriers and cultural differences I encountered at Beihang University are not hindrances but stepping stones to becoming a more versatile and adaptable individual. Approach each obstacle with an open mind and a willingness to learn, as the skills you develop will serve you well in both personal and professional future endeavors.

While focusing on academics is essential, building a strong network is equally important. Relationships are invaluable in both academic and professional growth. During my time at Beihang University, I met friends and partners who supported me personally and professionally, making a significant difference in my entrepreneurial journey. Networking should be a relentless pursuit—engage with classmates, professors, and alumni at every opportunity. These connections will form the foundation of your future success, opening doors and providing support as you navigate the complex landscape of entrepreneurship and international business.

Curiosity and a thirst for knowledge are essential qualities for any aspiring entrepreneur. The rapidly evolving technological landscape demands continuous education and learning. Stay abreast of the latest innovations in your field and beyond, constantly seeking out new information and perspectives. This commitment to lifelong learning will not only inform your business decisions but also position you as a leader in your industry, able to identify and capitalize on emerging trends. Enhance your professional skills during your time in China, as they will be crucial for your future success.

While it may seem daunting, taking calculated risks is crucial for unlocking remarkable opportunities. My decision to stay in China and start a business may have seemed like a significant leap, but it has the potential to lead me to remarkable achievements. Embrace the discomfort of stepping out of my comfort zone, as it is often in these moments of vulnerability that the greatest personal and professional growth occurs. Cultivate the resilience to weather the inevitable ups and downs of entrepreneurship, viewing setbacks as learning experiences that serve to strengthen my resolve. Make the most of your time studying and living in China, as it will equip you with a unique perspective and valuable experiences to draw from.

Contribute to the Belt and Road Initiative

China's visionary Belt and Road Initiative (BRI) has been instrumental in promoting global economic connectivity, and I am proud to participate in this transformative mission. The BRI's strategic focus on infrastructure development, trade facilitation, and foreign investment resonates. It fills me with hope and aspiration for the continued progress and prosperity of the Africa.

By leveraging the robust framework of the BRI, I can access wealthy resources and expansive networks that significantly strengthen my company's position and reach, both within China and on the global stage. This includes the ongoing partnership between China and Zambia, a key African partner in the BRI, which has unlocked new avenues for infrastructure investment, technological transfer, and economic cooperation.

I strongly encourage and empower other African entrepreneurs to proactively engage with the BRI, and enter China's dynamic markets through collaboration. With China's steadfast focus on fostering mutually beneficial partnerships and bolstering investment across Africa, I see the BRI as a transformative platform for driving economic progress that benefits both China and the African nations. By creating these vital conduits of collaboration, we can unlock unprecedented opportunities that uplift communities, foster sustainable development, and propel the shared vision of a more interconnected, prosperous world.

A Vision for Future Collaboration between China and Africa

Looking towards the future, I am deeply committed to promoting collaboration between China and Africa. This journey has illuminated the transformative power of cross-cultural exchange, and the profound impact it can have on both personal and professional growth. As my business continues to expand, I envision creating ever-greater opportunities for African countries to access the technological prowess and expertise that China offers, fostering a mutually beneficial cycle of economic and technological advancement.

I firmly believe that the vast market potential of Africa, coupled with China's enduring strengths in manufacturing and innovation, holds immense promise for the forging of impactful partnerships. My goal is to establish long-term, symbiotic collaborations that address the specific needs and challenges within key African industries, such as manufacturing, agriculture, and infrastructure. By drawing upon the solutions and best practices I have developed through my experiences in China, I aim to support the African continent's economic growth and development while enabling Chinese companies to tap into new and rapidly expanding markets.

I aspire to create a powerful catalyst for progress. My vision is to catalyze a virtuous cycle of knowledge sharing, technological transfer, and economic cooperation that empowers African nations to achieve greater self-sufficiency and prosperity while opening new frontiers for Chinese enterprises to thrive. By introducing advanced equipment, cutting-edge technologies and innovative business models, and bridging the strengths and resources of these two dynamic regions, I am confident that we can unlock unprecedented opportunities for shared prosperity and sustainable development.

Epilogue

If I could give my younger self some advice, I would say: Stand by your choices, and every mistake and decision has shaped who you are today. My journey of studying and entrepreneurship at Beihang University has been a transformative experience, filled with both challenges and remarkable opportunities. From navigating the unfamiliar as an international student, unsure of the language and customs, to now leading my own company in China, this path has been a crucible, forging my ability to thrive under pressure, seize strategic openings, and carve out my niche within a multicultural environment. The road ahead remains long and winding, but I am steadfast in my commitment to continually enhancing both myself and my company's capabilities. By offering quality services to an ever-expanding client base, I aspire to contribute meaningfully to the burgeoning economic cooperation between China and Africa.

This journey has given me the development space, shaped by the unique opportunities afforded to me through my Beihang University education and China's dynamic business landscape. With each step forward, I am driven to leverage my experiences and expertise to create a lasting impact, forging enduring bridges between my home continent and this remarkable country. To the esteemed institution of Beihang University, I extend my deepest gratitude for embarking upon this life-changing journey. And to China, the remarkable nation that has opened doors I had only dared to dream of, I offer my heartfelt appreciation. The future burns bright with promise, and I am eager to continue on this path of friendship, growth, and shared success, connecting China and Africa in ways that will resonate for generations to come.

Message from the Supervisor

As Musonda Stanley's supervisor, I am proud of his achievements in academics and entrepreneurship. His story is not only a symbol of personal striving but also a vivid portrayal of the friendship and cooperation between China and Africa. It is courage, wisdom, and persistence that enable him to shine in the communication of diverse cultures. I hope he will continue to embrace challenges with an open mind, use his talent and enthusiasm to build a bridge of communication between China and Africa, and contribute to the friendship and cooperation between the two countries.

Introduction to the Supervisor

Lin Feng is a professor under the "Outstanding Hundred Talents Program" of Beihang University, a doctoral supervisor, an Outstanding Young Talent in Beijing, and a Rising Star in Science and Technology in Beijing. He was selected as an outstanding young scholar of the Japan Society of Mechanical Engineers in 2011, a scholar of the Japan Society for the Promotion of Science (JSPS) in 2013, and a council member of the Technical Committee on Micro / Nano Robotics and Automation of the Institute of Electrical and Electronics Engineers (IEEE) in 2020. Currently, he serves as an editor of *Bio-Design and Manufacturing*, *Cyborg and Bionic Systems*, and *SmartBot*, and is also a council member of the Micro and Nano Robotics Branch and the Micro and Nano Manipulators and Actuators Branch of the Chinese Society of Micro-Nano Technology. He once served as an editorial board member and session chair of the CRA and the IROS. He has published more than 160 papers in SCI/EI indexed journals, such as *the International Journal of Robotics Research*, *Small*, *Research*, *Advanced Health Material*, *Advanced Intelligent System*, and *Lab on a Chip*. He has published 4 monographs including 1 chinese textbook titled *Introduction to Micro and Nanorobots* and 3 English monographs. He has won more than 30 provincial and ministerial-level awards and has applied for more than 40 patents.

Soar Dreams at Bei-
hang University: From
Vietnam to the Land of
Knowledge

05

北航让我腾飞梦想：从越南
飞往知识之地

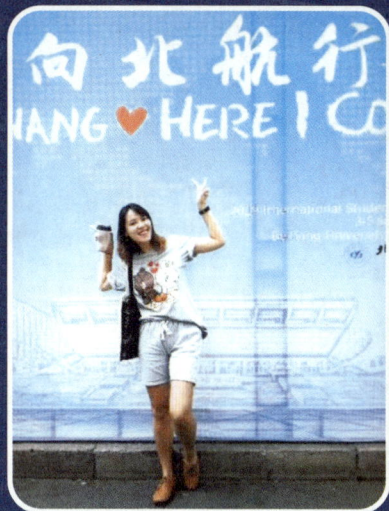

范秋燕

　　范秋燕（Yen Pham），来自越南。2019 年，怀揣着对金融领域的热爱与追求，她踏入了北航校园，成为金融硕士项目的一员。她在杨海军教授的指导下，深入研究股票价格预测模型，并成功完成了关于越南股票价格预测的论文。毕业后，她顺利获得了越南一家证券公司股权研究分析师的职位。为了进一步拓宽自己的职业边界，范秋燕不断寻求回到中国的机会。如今，她在上海的一家咨询公司担任商业分析师，专注于研究技术在金融服务转型中的应用，为越南企业的数字化转型提供宝贵的见解。

　　Yen Pham is from Vietnam. In 2019, with a passion and pursuit for the field of finance, she stepped onto the campus of Beihang University, becoming a member of the Master of Finance program. During her studies at Beihang University, under the guidance of Professor Haijun Yang, she delved into stock price prediction models and successfully completed her thesis on the prediction of Vietnamese stock prices. After graduation, she smoothly obtained a position as an equity research analyst at a Vietnamese securities firm. To further expand her career, Yen Pham continuously sought opportunities to return to China. Today, she works as a business analyst at a consulting firm in Shanghai, focusing on technology applications in the transformation of financial services and providing valuable insights for the digital transformation of Vietnamese enterprises.

扫码观看
采访视频

文化的吸引：从河内到北京的旅程

越南人对待其他文化的态度是真诚学习、友好相待。我们有韧性，对知识有不懈的追求。在我的成长过程中，中华文化特别吸引我。《西游记》《倚天屠龙记》等影视剧为我营造了一个充满冒险性和复杂性的生动世界。随着年龄的增长，我对中国历史和文化的好奇心与日俱增。我深入研究了《三国演义》《东周列国志》等中国著名文学作品。这些经典作品中王朝和文化的变迁故事，激励我去探索这个古老东方文明对越南的文化产生了怎样的影响。

在大学的第二年，我做出了一个重要决定：开始学习汉语。正是这个决定使我的生活发生了巨大变化，它不仅使我对中华文化和中国人民有了更深的理解，也使我的人生轨迹从此转向。我的汉语老师是一位充满激情的教育工作者，作为国际学生，她在北京的经历就像灯塔一样，给了懵懂的我清晰的指引。她在中国的生活故事，描绘出了一个现代化国家的图景。在汉语课上，她的热情非常感染人。她分享的不仅仅是对语言的见解，还有对生活方式、文化环境以及那仿佛遥遥等待着我的精彩国际学生生活的见解。她激发了我出国留学的想法，让我意识到，留学中国不仅仅是获得学术成就的机会，也是拓宽视野的机会，更是我融入长期以来向往的文化的机会。"去那片历史深厚和创新涌现的土地上继续我的教育！"在这个想法的召唤下，我踏上了塑造我的职业道路和个人成长历程的旅程。

我决定飞向知识的新天地，于是我选择了北航。北航以其严谨的学术探索和创新研究而闻名遐迩。此外，北航位于中国的首都，这样的战略位置，为我融入世界经济网络提供了无与伦比的机会。在汉语老师的支持和建议下，我如愿以偿申请到了中国政府奖学金并被北航录取。在北航的求学道路不仅丰富了我的生活，还增强了我对教育和文化交流力量的信念。希望分享我的故事，能激励其他学生追求自己的梦想，迎接新挑战，跨越国界，发现新世界。

难忘的第一印象

抵达中国时，我的第一感受是兴奋带着敬畏。刚下飞机，我就被一种

弥漫在城市中的活力所包围。熙熙攘攘的街
道、精美的建筑以及当地人温暖的微笑，立
刻让我有受到欢迎的感觉。走在长安街上，
我能感受到辉煌历史与现代文明的交融。
我参观了故宫、天坛和长城等标志性建筑，
这些建筑是文化的象征，也是我了解中国
的重要窗口，让我明白历史是如何塑造今
天中国人的思想和生活方式。我开始领悟
中华文化中蕴含的价值观，例如家庭观念、
尊重长辈和对教育的重视等。

在长城上留影

　　北航本身同样令人印象深刻。从我踏
入校园的那一刻起，现代化的设施和浓厚
的学术氛围便深深吸引了我。国际学生的迎新活动组织得非常周到，帮助我
轻松适应新环境。我迅速与来自不同背景的同学建立了联系，这进一步丰富
了我的经历。

梦想成真：在北航的成长

　　在我入学国际学院的那一天，我有幸结识了来自五大洲的同学。我与
来自尼日利亚、巴基斯坦、俄罗斯和土耳其等国的学生交流，被他们的文化
和语言所吸引。国际学生的宿舍是一个充满活力的社区，我们经常聚在一起。
宿舍的共享空间成了文化交流的中心，我们组织聚会，展示和分享各自国家
的特色菜肴。生活在这里就像置身于一个微型世界，每一天都让我"飞"往
一个新的国家，体验不同的文化。这种多元文化环境不仅丰富了我对世界的
理解，还让我的适应能力变得更强。与这样一个多样化的群体互动，使我获
得了未来在跨国工作环境中非常有用的技能，这也凸显了在互联互通的世界
中，合作和文化共享的重要性。

　　我参与了多项活动，以便更深入地了解中国历史和文化。这些活动让
我对传统中国节日、习俗和艺术形式有了更深刻的理解。例如，我参加了春
节庆祝活动，学习书法和包饺子。这些活动让我不仅沉浸在节日氛围中，还

意识到文化交流的重要性。我发现，了解一个国家的历史和文化不仅能帮助我更好地融入这个环境，还能丰富我的学术研究。

我的思维方式与问题解决方法也发生了重大转变，其中最显著的变化体现在学业上。在我之前的大学学习里，我只是被动地吸收教授们讲解的知识和理论，而在这里，我必须在每节课前进行研究，熟悉课堂主题，以便在课堂上展示自己的理解和想法。每一节课都是学生与教授之间的互动讨论，老师鼓励我们积极参与，我们学习和探讨的内容远远超出了课本。这种互动式的学习方法不仅增强了我对信息的记忆能力，还激发了我深入研究课题的好奇心，我不再像以前那样仅仅被动地接受灌输。在北航的学习经历显著提高了我的自学和研究能力，使我掌握了有效的方法来面对和解决问题。这些技能在我目前担任咨询公司业务分析师的工作中发挥了重要作用。北航的教授们给我们传授了各个行业的实践经验，他们在课堂上分享实际案例，带学生进行案例研究，帮助我清晰地规划未来的职业道路，并使我具备职场技能，来追求成为金融顾问或咨询师的理想。

范秋萍（右三）在北航体验中华文化

北航所学显著拓宽了我对金融领域趋势变化的视野。如果没有在北航的学术旅程，我可能根本不知道定量金融的存在。定量金融的一个应用是机器人顾问（Robo-Advisors），在了解这一领域并考虑越南金融行业的现状后，我受到启发，创造性地提出一个针对越南金融市场的 Robo-Advisors 概念。我与我的姐姐合作，参加了由住友集团组织的 Startup 101 竞赛，展示了我们关于个人财务顾问的想法。我们的提案入围前五名，并且有机会向住友集团的高层领导汇报。尽管最终我们的创意没有被选中，但参与这次竞赛极大地丰富了我的经验。我将这次的灵感归功于北航，是北航对我的创意形成起到了关键作用。

总体而言，我在中国，尤其是北航的经历不仅满足了我的期望，更超出了我的期望。严谨的学术研究氛围与沉浸式文化环境相结合，为我提供了一个独特的平台。我发现，在中国学习到的不仅仅是知识，更是如何理解不同视角并建立起跨越国界的持久关系。这段旅程确实具有变革性，塑造了我的世界观，并激励我对未来的追求。

对导师的衷心感谢

在我的学术旅程中，我的导师杨海军教授在金融领域的知识，尤其是在股票预测方面的专业性，有效帮助了我的研究。他还激励我对复杂的金融概念进行批判性和创造性的思考。杨教授对专业的热情体现在每一堂课中，他还为我的论文提出了宝贵的反馈意见，帮助我完

硕士学位论文答辩现场

善想法并建立了一个稳健的分析框架。他的支持不仅提升了我的研究技能，也培养了我的自信，这种自信延续到了我的职业生涯中。

知识的桥梁：连接中国与越南

我现在在上海一家咨询公司担任业务分析师，主要负责研究银行业的最新技术和发展。在这个职位上，我深入分析前沿技术，以及中国的银行如何利用移动银行服务庞大的客户。基于我对中国市场的研究，我能够为越南银行的数字化转型提供有价值的建议，提升客户体验。我还与中国企业合作，推动他们在越南的投资。我研究最新政策，利用对越南当地情况的了解调查越南的商业环境、法律框架，以有效指导希望进入越南市场的中国投资者。中国的科技在快速发展，我有幸亲身体验了银行业的重塑和创新过程，可以为中国投资者提供有见地的咨询，并帮助他们理解越南市场的增长潜力，建立两国企业之间的合作伙伴关系。

在上海黄浦江边小憩

范秋燕（右一）与工作伙伴

在中国生活使我沉浸在一个崇尚创新的文化中，上海快节奏的氛围和在全球金融中心的生活体验丰富了我，使我拥有了全球化的思维视角。我很骄傲能利用我在北航获得的知识来支持自己国家银行业的数字化转型。我希望能够继续提升自己的专业技能，在金融领域取得更大的成绩。同时，我也希望能够与北航保持联系，为母校的发展贡献自己的一份力量。我期待着有一天能够回到北航，看看那些熟悉的校园角落，和曾经的老师、同学重逢。

对国际学生的建议

对于那些考虑来北航留学的人，我想说，这里不仅是追求学术的中心，也是自我探索和全球参与的平台。北航拥有一流的师资力量和丰富的学术资源，教授们具有深厚的专业知识，并关心学生的发展。他们鼓励我们提出问题，挑战传统思维，为我们创造了一个开放的学习环境，使我们能够充分发挥潜力。

此外，北航位于北京这座国际大都市，能提供无与伦比的实习和就业机会。在这里，你有机会与来自世界各地的同学互动，建立跨文化友谊，拓宽视野。无论你对金融、工程还是其他领域感兴趣，北航都能为你提供充足的平台。

总之，如果你渴望在一个充满活力和创新精神的环境中学习，同时深入了解中国丰富的历史和文化，那么北航将是你理想的选择。我衷心希望更多的国际学生能够和我一样，在留学的道路上收获满满，实现自己的梦想。

导师寄语

　　作为范秋燕的硕士指导教师，我为她在北航和在工作中获得的成就感到无比自豪。她的努力和才华将在多变的行业发展中绽放出耀眼的光芒。我希望她在工作中继续保持对学习的渴望和对挑战的热忱，以开放的心态迎接每一个新的机遇。我想对她说：你所从事的咨询领域不仅是个人职业发展的平台，更是推动中越合作的前沿阵地。在全球化的进程中，请你尽情发挥你的智慧与创造力，积极促进不同文化之间的交流与理解。我相信，你将用你的热情和专注，架起中越友谊的桥梁，为两国的合作作出贡献。无论未来的道路如何，我都会为你加油，期待看到你在职业生涯中不断突破自我，续写辉煌篇章。

　　祝你一切顺利，前程似锦！

导师简介

　　杨海军，北航经济管理学院教授，博士生导师。Fulbright 学者，北航人文社科首批拔尖人才。主要研究方向有分布式计算、进化算法、Fintech 金融大数据、计算金融、行为金融、高频市场交易等。项目"进化计算理论及应用研究"获 2007 年教育部自然科学奖一等奖（第四完成人）。在 *Decision Support Systems*、*International Review of Financial Analysis*、*Journal of Behavioral Finance*、*Research in International Business and Finance*、*International Journal of Finance & Economics*、《中国科学》、《计算机学报》、《自动化学报》、《管理科学学报》、《管理评论》、《财贸经济》、等国内外期刊上，发表论文 50 余篇。

The Allure of Culture: A Journey from Hanoi to Beijing

My fellow Vietnamese are hardworking, genuinely interested in other cultures, and friendly. Our culture emphasizes resilience and a relentless pursuit of knowledge. As I grew up, I was particularly attracted by the charm of Chinese culture. Iconic films such as *Journey to the West*, *The Heaven Sword and Dragon Saber* played a significant role in this fascination, offering me a glimpse into a vibrant world filled with adventure and complexity. As I grew older, my curiosity deepened. I delved into renowned Chinese literary works like *Romance of the Three Kingdoms* and *Chronicles of Eastern Zhou Kingdoms*. These narratives, filled with tales of dynasties and cultural transformations, inspired me to explore the ancient civilization that has influenced our culture.

In my second year at university, I took a pivotal step: I began learning Chinese. This decision marked a turning point in my life, providing me with a deeper understanding of the culture and its people. My Chinese teacher, a passionate educator with her own experiences as an international student in Beijing, became a beacon of inspiration. Her stories of life in China painted a vivid picture of a modern country. In each class, her enthusiasm was infectious. She shared insights not just about the language but also about the lifestyle, the cultural environment, and the vibrant community of international students that awaited me. Her encouragement fueled my desire to study abroad, to immerse myself in an environment that promised growth and discovery. I realized that studying in China was not just about academic achievement. It would also be an opportunity to broaden my horizons and engage with a culture that had long intrigued me. The idea of continuing my education in a land so rich in history and innovation felt like a calling, leading me on a journey that would ultimately shape my career and personal growth.

With the decision to fly to new horizons of knowledge, I chose Beihang University. Beihang University is renowned for its rigorous academic and innovative research. Moreover, Beihang University's advantageous location in

China's capital provides unparalleled opportunities for networking and internships in one of the world's largest economies. With the support and advice from my Chinese teacher, I applied for the CSC scholarship and was selected by Beihang University. My study journey at Beihang University has not only enriched my life but also reinforced my belief in the power of education and cultural exchange. As I share my story, I hope to inspire others to pursue their dreams, embrace new challenges, and discover the world beyond their borders.

The Unforgettable First Impression

Upon my arrival in China, my first impression was a blend of excitement and awe. The moment I stepped off the plane, I was surrounded by a sense of energy that permeated the city. The bustling streets, the intricate architecture, and the warm smiles of the locals immediately made me feel welcomed. Walking along Chang'an Avenue, I could almost feel the grandeur of great history blending with modern civilization. Iconic landmarks, such as the Forbidden City, the Temple of Heaven, and the Great Wall, are not only symbols of culture but also important windows through which I was able to understand more about China and how history has shaped the thoughts and lifestyle of the Chinese people today. I began to grasp the values embedded in Chinese culture, such as family orientation, respect for elders, and the emphasis on education.

Beihang University itself was equally impressive. From the moment I arrived on campus, I was struck by its modern facilities and its spirit of academic excellence. The orientation activities for international students were thoughtfully organized, helping me to navigate my new environment with ease. I quickly connected with fellow students from diverse backgrounds, which enriched my experience further.

Realize Dreams: Growth at Beihang University

On the day of my enrollment at the International School, I had the incredible opportunity to meet and forge friendships with peers worldwide. I connected with students from Nigeria, Pakistan, Russia, Turkey and other countries, and was fascinated by their culture and languages. Living in the same dormitory created a vibrant community where international students frequently gathered. Our shared space became a hub of cultural exchange, where we organized meetings to showcase and share typical dishes from our home countries. It felt like living in a miniature world, where each day allowed me to "travel" to a new country and experience a different culture. This multicultural environment has not only enriched my understanding of the world but also made me more adaptable. Engaging with such a diverse group of individuals has equipped me with skills in a multinational work setting in the future, and highlighted the importance of collaboration and cultural appreciation in a interconnected world.

I participated in several activities to learn more about Chinese history and culture. These activities allowed me to gain a deeper understanding of traditional Chinese festivals, customs, and art forms. For example, I took part in the Spring Festival celebrations and learned to practice calligraphy and make dumplings. These activities not only immersed me in the festive atmosphere but also made me realize the importance of cultural exchange. I found that understanding a country's history and culture not only helps me integrate better into this environment but also enriches my academic research.

My perspective and approach to solving problems marked a significant shift. One of the most noticeable changes was in my educational experience. At my previous university, I passively absorbed knowledge and theories presented by my professors. But here, we were expected to research and familiarize ourselves with the topics before each class, allowing us to present our own interpretations and insights. Each class felt like an engaging discussion between students and professors, encouraging active participation. The learning contents extended far beyond the books. This interactive learning method not only enhanced my retention of information but also ignited my curiosity to delve deeper into subjects rather than merely receive knowledge passively. The educational process at

Beihang University has significantly improved my self-study and research skills, equipping me with effective methods for approaching and solving problems. These skills have proven invaluable in my current work as a business analyst in a consulting firm.The professors brought a wealth of practical experience from their work in various industries. Their real-world examples and case studies in class helped me visualize potential career paths and clarified the specific skills I needed to pursue my ambition of becoming a financial advisor or consultant.

Beihang University has significantly broadened my horizons regarding the trends and changes in the field of finance, which I am currently pursuing. Without my academic journey at Beihang University, I may not have even been aware of the existence of quantitative finance. One exciting application of quantitative finance is the creation of Robo-Advisors. Upon discovering this field and considering the state of the financial industry in Vietnam, I was inspired to develop the concept of a Robo-Advisor tailored for the Vietnamese market. I collaborated with my sister to enter the Startup 101 competition organized by the Sumitomo Group, presenting our idea for a Personal Financial Consultant. Our proposal was shortlisted among the top 5, which allowed us to showcase it to senior leaders at Sumitomo Group in Japan. Although our idea was not selected for final investment, participating in this competition enriched my experience tremendously. I owe this inspiration to Beihang University, which has been instrumental in shaping my ideas and providing valuable experiences.

Overall, my experiences in China and at Beihang University have not only met but surpassed my expectations. The combination of rigorous academic research atmosphere and culturally immersive environment has provided me with a unique platform. I have found that studying in China is not just about knowledge; it is about understanding different perspectives and building lasting relationships that transcend borders. This journey has truly been transformative, shaping my worldview and fueling my aspirations for the future.

Big Thanks to My Supervisor

Throughout my academic journey, Professor Haijun Yang, my thesis advisor, has deep expertise in finance, especially in stock forecasting. He not only guided my research but also inspired me to think critically and creatively about complex financial concepts. Professor Yang's passion for his field was evident in every lecture, and he provided invaluable feedback on my thesis and helped me refine my ideas and develop a robust analytical framework. His support not only enhanced my research skills but also instilled in me a sense of confidence that has been carried over into my professional life.

A Bridge of Knowledge: Connect China and Vietnam

Currently, I am working as a business analyst for a consulting firm in Shanghai, where my primary responsibility is to research the latest technologies and advancements in the banking industry. In my position, I conduct in-depth analyses of cutting-edge technologies and how banks in China use mobile banking solutions to serve a large number of customers. Based on my research of the Chinese market, I can provide valuable insight for Vietnamese banks on their digital transformation journey and enhance their customer experience. I also work with Chinese firms to promote their investments in Vietnam. With my local knowledge, I conduct research on Vietnam's latest policies and investigate the business environment, legal landscape in Vietnam, to effectively guide Chinese investors to expand into the Vietnamese market. Given China's rapid technological development, I have been fortunate to witness and experience firsthand the innovations that are reshaping the banking industry. This exposure enables me to provide informed consultations to Chinese investors, helping them understand the potential for growth in Vietnam and the kinds of partnerships that can be fostered between our two countries.

Living in China has been a precious experience, allowing me to immerse myself in a culture that thrives on innovation. The fast-paced environment of

Shanghai, combined with its status as a global financial hub, has enriched my personal life, enabling me to think with a global vision. I am proud to utilize the knowledge I learned to support the digital transformation of Vietnam's banking industry, and I hope to continue improving my professional skills and making greater achievements in the financial sector. I wish to keep in contact with Beihang University, making my own contribution to my alma mater. I look forward to coming back to the campus one day in the future, walking around the places I'm familiar with, and meeting the teachers and friends again.

Advice for International Students

To those considering studying at Beihang University, I want to say that this place is not only a hub for excellence academic but also a platform for self-exploration and global engagement. Beihang University boasts top-notch faculty and abundant academic resources. Its professors possess deep expertise and are genuinely concerned about students' development. They encourage us to ask questions and challenge conventional thinking, creating an open learning environment that allows us to fully unleash my potential.

Moreover, Beihang University is located in Beijing, an international metropolis, provides unparalleled internship and employment opportunities. Here, you will have the chance to interact with classmates from around the world, build cross-cultural friendships, and broaden your horizons. Whether you are interested in finance, engineering, or other fields, Beihang University can offer you ample platforms.

In summary, if you are eager to learn in a vibrant and innovative environment while delving into China's rich history and culture, Beihang University is your ideal choice. I sincerely hope that international students will have a rewarding academic journey and fulfill their dreams, just as I achieved along the way.

Message from the Supervisor

As the supervisor of Yen Pham, I am immensely proud of her achievements both at Beihang University and during her work. Her dedication and talent will undoubtedly shine brightly in this ever-changing industry. I hope she continues to maintain her thirst for learning and passion for tackling challenges, embracing each new opportunity with an open mind. I have a few words for her: The consulting work you are engaged in is not only a platform for personal career development but also a frontline for advancing cooperation between China and Vietnam. In the process of globalization, please use your intellect and creativity to actively promote cultural exchange and mutual understanding. I firmly believe that with your enthusiasm and focus, you can build bridges of friendship between China and Vietnam and make contributions to collaboration between the two nations. No matter where the future takes you, I will always cheer you on, eagerly looking forward to seeing you push your boundaries and write new chapters of success in your career.

Wishing you all the best and a bright future ahead!

Introduction to the Supervisor

Haijun Yang is a professor and doctoral supervisor at the School of Economics and Management, Beihang University. He is a Fulbright scholar and one of the first batch of top talents in humanities and social sciences at Beihang University. His main research directions include distributed computing, evolutionary algorithms, Fintech financial big data, computational finance, behavioral finance, high-frequency market trading, etc. The project Research on the Theory and Application of Evolutionary Computation won the first prize of the Natural Science Award of the Ministry of Education in 2007 (the fourth contributor). He has published more than 50 papers in journals such as

Decision Support Systems, International Review of Financial Analysis, Journal of Behavioral Finance, Research in International Business and Finance, International Journal of Finance & Economics, Science China, Chinese Journal of Computers, Acta Automatica Sinica, Journal of Management Sciences in China, Management Review, Finance & Trade Economics.

06

跨越半球的 "AI 奇遇"

李 威

　　李威（Edwin Trejo），来自秘鲁，2015年，他带着对机械电子工程的热爱与梦想，踏入了北航，开始了他的硕士学习。经过三年的勤奋努力，李威以优异的成绩获得了硕士学位。毕业后，他加入北京一家人工智能（AI）公司，开启了职业生涯的新篇章。2021年，李威搬至广州，担任高级AI研究工程师，专注于大语言模型方向的研究与开发，并在交通领域展现了出色的专业能力和创新思维。

　　Edwin Trejo is from Peru. Driven by his passion and dreams for mechatronic engineering, Edwin stepped onto the campus of Beihang University and began his study for a master's degree in 2015. After three years of diligent efforts, he obtained his master's degree with excellent grades. After graduation, he joined an AI company in Beijing, kicking off a new chapter in his career. In 2021, Edwin moved to Guangzhou. He serves as a senior AI research engineer, focusing on researching and developing large language models (LLMs). He has demonstrated outstanding professional capabilities and innovative thinking in the transportation field.

扫码观看
采访视频

我是李威，来自秘鲁。我的追梦旅程跨越了文化和地理的界限，证明了不懈努力就可以成就卓越。身为秘鲁的青年，我对科技和工程抱有无比的热忱，这份热爱驱使我远赴中国求学，开启了一段充满挑战与成长的学习之旅。

从适应到突破

2015 年，我踏入了北航的大门，正式开始了我的机械电子工程专业硕士研究生的学习。这次跨越重洋的求学之旅，对我来说，不仅是学术上的巨大挑战，更是一次深刻的文化洗礼。初抵北京，这座繁华大都市的壮丽景象深深震撼了我，熙熙攘攘的街道、蓬勃发展的科技氛围以及截然不同的生活节奏，都让我意识到这里与秘鲁有着天壤之别。这并未让我感到丝毫退缩，反而点燃了我内心深处的奋斗热情。

李威的硕士毕业照

最初几个月，我投入了大量精力去适应这个全新的环境。语言是我面临的首要挑战。尽管在秘鲁时我已经掌握了一些基础的汉语知识，但把这些知识实际应用在日常生活和学习中却非常困难。与教授在课堂上交流时，与同学进行学术讨论时，我都深感自己要加倍努力才能跟上大家的节奏。因此，我下定决心要提升自己的汉语水平。我在课余时间参加学校的语言课程，与同学们练习口语，观看中国的新闻节目和影视作品，以此来进一步熟悉语言环境。

我的研究方向是人机交互，这是一个融合了机械电子、计算机编程、AI 以及信号处理等多个学科的领域，对我来说，这无疑是一场全方位的考验。但我从未有过退缩的念头，这种跨学科的挑战反而让我的学习生活变得异常丰富和充实。在学习过程中，我逐渐将各个学科的知识融合起来，并不断思考如何利用科技的力量来改善人类的生活。

跨界融合与成长

　　2016 年，我有幸遇到了我的导师袁培江副教授。袁教授是北航人机交互领域的领军人物，他不仅学术造诣深厚，科研经验也极为丰富。初次见面时，我就被他渊博的知识和严谨的治学态度所折服。袁教授非常认可我的学术热情和求知欲，因此让我加入了他的研究团队，专注于研究基于 Kinect 设备的姿势识别。在这个项目中，我负责研究如何利用 Kinect 传感器的深度摄像头捕捉人体的运动轨迹，并通过算法分析来识别不同的瑜伽姿势。Kinect 原本是一种用于游戏领域的设备，但我希望通过技术创新，将其应用于更广泛的健康与健身领域。这个想法得到了袁教授的支持，并最终成为我硕士论文的研究内容。

　　为了攻克技术难题，我不断学习更复杂的算法和编程技术。我深入研究了计算机视觉领域的前沿技术，查阅了大量相关文献，并与团队中的其他成员一起探讨解决方案。经过无数个夜晚的努力，我终于在算法准确度和识别速度上取得了显著进展，成功设计出了一套能够精确识别不同瑜伽动作的系统。2018 年，我的研究成果在先进机器人与机电一体化国际会议（ICARM）和机器人与自动化科学国际会议（ICRAS）上得到发表，引起学术界的广泛关注。我的研究不仅展示了 Kinect 在非游戏领域的应用潜力，也为人机交互系统的研究开辟了新的方向。

参加国际学术会议

　　这些学术会议让我收获颇丰，它们让我有了与全球顶尖的学者深入交流的机会，并极大地拓展了我的国际视野。即使在学业中取得了一定的成绩，我也没有因此而停下脚步。真正的科学技术交流，乃是美美与共的过程，文化的传播与交流亦是如此。为了向更多的中国人展示秘鲁丰富的文化与美食，我积极参加大学的国际文化节。在活动中，我精心组织了秘鲁文化的展示，准备了各种传统美食，并

李威（右二）与朋友们游览多个城市

向来宾们详细讲解秘鲁的历史与习俗。秘鲁距离中国较远，许多中国人对这个国家并不熟悉，因此这个活动是一个绝佳的契机，我不仅让大家享受到美味的食物，更促进了中秘文化的交流。

我去了中国多个城市旅行，深入了解中国的历史、文化和人民。在西安，我看到了举世闻名的兵马俑，深切感受到了古老文明的博大精深；在上海，我体验了现代化都市的繁华，领略了国际大都市的风采；在桂林，我放慢了脚步，徜徉在山水之间，享受那片让无数人心驰神往的美丽景色。这些旅行不仅丰富了我的学识，更让我深刻体会到中国这片土地的多样性与独特性，让我对这片土地充满了热爱与敬畏。

在我的学生生涯即将画上句号之际，袁教授又给予了我一个宝贵的建议，他推荐我加入北京一家正处于快速发展阶段的 AI 公司。这家公司专注于 AI 技术的前沿研究与应用，可以为我提供一个施展才华的广阔舞台。进入公司后，我积极参与了多个项目的研发工作。特别是在基于足迹与鞋印测量关系的研究中，我利用卷积神经网络来计算身高，还负责了自动售货机日常消费品的检测项目，针对 20 种产品优化了多目标检测的 YOLOv3 模型。在这些项目中，我充分发挥在学术研究中培养出来的创新思维，为公司开发出多个具有市场竞争力的智能系统解决方案。

新的挑战与展望

　　2021 年，我决定接受新的挑战，搬至广州，加入在 AI 领域享有盛誉的佳都科技。这家公司专注于智能交通、智慧城市等领域的技术创新，其企业文化强调创新和团队合作，这与我的个人追求不谋而合。我渴望通过自己的研究为城市的交通问题提供智能化解决方案。在佳都科技，我主要负责大语言模型的研究工作，这是一种用于自然语言处理的深度学习模型。大语言模型的发展标志着 AI 领域的一个重要突破，它使得机器能够更准确地理解和生成人类语言。加入公司的第一年，我就带领团队将技术转化为切实可行的解决方案，研发了一个名为 TransGPT 的语言模型，这个模型是专为交通行业设计的，能够利用大数据分析交通流量、预测拥堵情况。通过对数据的分析和对模型的不断优化，我们实现了交通流量的精准预测与智能调度，TransGPT 为多个城市的交通管理提供了科学依据，解决了城市交通管理中的诸多痛点。

　　我还参与了与华为团队的合作项目，致力于将大语言模型的计算需求与华为的昇腾计算平台相结合。昇腾计算平台是华为推出的 AI 计算平台，旨在为 AI 应用提供强大的计算支持。我与华为团队紧密合作，共同探讨如

李威（右一）和同事们

何通过量化技术优化大语言模型，使其在昇腾计算平台上能够高效运行。这一过程中，我充分发挥了自己在机器学习和算法优化方面的特长，为昇腾计算平台的技术进步贡献了自己的力量。这次合作项目的成功，不仅让佳都科技在智能交通领域的技术优势得到进一步巩固，也让我在公司和行业内赢得了更多的认可。我的研究成果为推动交通领域的智能化发展提供了新的技术支撑，也为大语言模型在实际应用中的可扩展性开辟了新的探索方向。

我不断思考着科技与人们生活之间的关系，不仅关注技术在各个行业中的应用，更希望技术能够真正服务社会，造福人类。我坚信，AI 的进步绝不仅仅是技术层面的突破，它还将对社会运作、城市管理和人们的生活方式产生深远影响。因此，我将自己的工作重心放在了对智能交通和智慧城市的研究上，期望通过 AI 的力量，缓解交通拥堵，降低碳排放，提升城市的运营效率。

我明白我取得的这一切成绩与我在北航的学习经历密不可分。那段学习经历让我打下了扎实的工程基础，学会了如何进行跨学科的研究，更让我懂得学术的意义不仅仅在于解决问题，更在于拓宽思维，推动社会进步。我时常回想起在北航的日子，特别是与我的导师袁教授共度的时光。袁教授不仅传授了我专业知识，更重要的是，他让我成为一个有责任感的研究者，教会我如何将理论与实践相结合，为社会创造价值。我深知自己的成功并非仅仅依靠个人的努力，更有师长和朋友们的无私帮助与支持。因此，我在工作中始终保持着开放的心态，乐于接纳他人的意见与建议，尊重每一个与我共事的人。同时，我也努力将自己的知识与经验分享给更多的年轻人，希望能帮助他们少走弯路，早日找到成功的道路。

AI 领域的技术前沿不断更新，业内竞争日益激烈，作为一名高级 AI 研究员，这些让我的生活充满了挑战与机遇。但我始终保持着谦逊和务实的态度，无论面临多大的压力，我都保持着对科技的热情和解决问题的耐心。我坚信，只要付出足够的努力，就一定能获得回报。虽然工作时很紧绷，但我的生活也是丰富多彩的。我特别喜欢中国的美食，总是尝试各种地方的特色菜肴。从北京的炸酱面到广州的早茶，从四川的麻辣火锅到东北的酸菜炖白肉，这些食物让我感受到中国各地的独特风情。

如果用两个关键词来概括我的故事，我想会是奋斗和成就。一个外国学生通过不懈努力，在中国这片广袤的土地上找到自己的位置，然后利用科技的力量推动社会发展，提升人们的生活质量。无论是在学习还是工作中，我都始终保持对科技的热爱，对生活的热情，以及对未来的坚定信心。如今，我站在 AI 研究与开发的最前沿，致力于进一步优化和应用大语言模型。展望未来，我满怀希望，我深信随着技术的持续进步，AI 将在越来越多的领域中展现其重要性。我渴望通过自己的努力，进一步推动 AI 技术在各行各业的应用，特别是在智能交通、智慧城市等领域，助力更多城市实现智能化管理，为人们的生活带来实质性的改善，为全球智能化的发展贡献自己的一份力量。同时，我也期待在未来的工作中，继续与全球顶尖的学者和企业携手推动科技进步。

　　我的故事，是关于不懈追梦的故事。我从秘鲁来到中国，克服了文化与语言的重重障碍，攀登过学术的高峰，如今置身于充满挑战与机遇的职业生涯中。无论是在学术研究，还是在工作岗位中，我始终保持着严谨的态度和无畏的精神，不断迎接新的挑战，超越自己。我的故事仍在继续，无论未来的道路多么崎岖，我都会以坚定的步伐，勇往直前，搏出一个光明的未来。

导师寄语

李威的研究生阶段，正逢 3D 视觉和 AI 的兴起。他尝试将 Kinect 用于瑜伽教学并取得了卓越的成绩。我为他的创新精神感到无比骄傲。他在行业内 AI 算法应用方面的表现十分优异，不仅掌握了复杂的理论，还将其转化为实际的解决方案，推动了创新与进步。

他在北航的学习专注而勤奋。这只是开始，他所习得的知识与技能是他探索世界的工具。愿他满怀信心地前行，继续探索 AI 的巨大潜力，在全球舞台上产生更大的影响。愿他的旅程满是成功与收获！

导师简介

袁培江，北航机械工程及自动化学院副教授、硕士生导师。在国内外知名期刊和会议上发表论文 50 余篇，其中 SCI、EI、ISTP 收录 30 余篇。承担多项与智能控制和具身智能机器人相关的跨学科研究课题，参与"机电控制工程技术双语教学"教改项目。积极参与国家自然科学基金重大项目、973 计划等国家重大项目的申报。曾任 ICRA 2011、IROS 2011 大会委员会副主编、WCICA 2010 大会分会主席、ICIEA 2014 大会分会主席、IJARS（SCI 期刊）编委、863 先进制造专家组秘书等。

I am Edwin Trejo, from Peru. My journey of pursuing dreams has crossed cultural and geographical boundaries, proving that relentless efforts can lead to extraordinary achievements. As a young Peruvian passionate about technology and engineering, my enthusiasm drove me to study in China, embarking on a journey filled with challenges and growth.

From Adaptation to Breakthrough

In 2015, I entered Beihang University to pursue a master's degree in Mechatronic Engineering. This overseas study journey was not only a huge academic challenge for me but also a profound cultural immersion. Upon arriving in Beijing, the magnificent scenery of this bustling metropolis left a deep impression on me. The bustling streets, the vibrant atmosphere of technological development, and the vastly different pace of life all made me realize how profoundly different it was from Peru. This did not intimidate me, instead, it ignited a deep sense of determination within me.

In the first few months, I devoted a lot of energy to adapting to this new environment. Language was my primary challenge. Although I had already acquired some basic Chinese back in Peru, applying this knowledge in daily life and academic was quite difficult. Whether communicating with professors during lectures or participating in academic discussions with classmates, I often felt the need to work twice as hard to keep up. Determined to improve, I resolved to enhance my Chinese skills by attending language courses at the university, practicing conversational skills with peers, and watching Chinese news programs and TV shows to immerse myself further in the language.

My research focused on human-computer interaction, a multidisciplinary field integrating mechatronics, computer programming, artificial intelligence, and signal processing. For me, this was undoubtedly a comprehensive test. Yet, I never considered giving up. Instead, this interdisciplinary challenge made my academic life exceptionally enriching and fulfilling. Throughout my studies, I gradually integrated knowledge from various disciplines and continuously pondered how to harness the power of technology to improve human life.

Cross-border Integration and Growth

In 2016, I was fortunate to meet my supervisor, Associate Professor Peijiang Yuan. Professor Yuan is a leading figure in the field of human-computer interaction at Beihang University and is known for his profound academic expertise and extensive research experience. When we first met, I was deeply impressed by his vast knowledge and rigorous academic attitude. Recognizing my passion for learning and my thirst for knowledge, Professor Yuan invited me to join his research team to focus on gesture recognition research using Kinect devices. In this project, I was responsible for exploring how to use the depth camera of the Kinect sensor to capture human motion trajectories and analyze these data through algorithms to recognize different yoga poses. Although Kinect was originally a device used in the gaming field, I hoped to extend its use to broader fields, particularly health and fitness, through technological innovation. This idea earned Professor Yuan's support and ultimately became the focus of my master's thesis.

To overcome technical challenges, I continuously learned to master more complex algorithms and programming techniques. I delved deeply into cutting-edge technologies in the field of computer vision, consulted a vast amount of related literature, and collaborated with other team members to brainstorm solutions. After countless nights of effort, I finally achieved significant progress in both algorithm accuracy and recognition speed, successfully designing a system capable of accurately identifying various yoga poses. My research results were published at the ICARM 2018 and ICRAS 2018, attracting significant attention from the academic community. My research not only demonstrated the potential of Kinect in non-gaming applications but also opened up new directions for research in human-computer interaction systems.

These academic conferences were immensely rewarding, offering me the opportunity to engage in depth discussions with leading scholars worldwide and greatly broadening my international perspective. Even though I achieved certain academic milestones, I never allowed myself to become complacent. I realized that the essence of science and technology lies in mutual learning and exchange, which also extends to cultural dissemination and dialogues. To showcase the rich culture and cuisine of Peru to more Chinese people, I actively participated in the International Cultural Festival held by my university. During the event, I carefully organized a presentation on Peruvian culture, prepared various traditional dishes, and provided detailed explanations of Peru's history and customs to the guests. Since Peru is geographically distant from China, many Chinese are not familiar with this country. So, this event served as an excellent opportunity for people to enjoy delicious food and a bridge for Sino-Peruvian cultural exchanges.

I traveled to many cities, gaining a deep understanding of Chinese history, culture, and people. In Xi'an, I toured the world-famous Terracotta Warriors, experiencing the profound richness of ancient civilization. In Shanghai, I marveled at the vibrancy and prosperity of a modern metropolis, witnessing the charm of an international city. In Guilin, I slowed down and wandered among the mountains and rivers, enjoying the breathtaking scenery that has captivated countless hearts. These travels not only enriched my knowledge but also made me deeply appreciate the diversity and uniqueness of China, filling me with love and awe for it.

As my student career drew to a close, Professor Yuan gave me another valuable suggestion. He recommended that I join a rapidly developing artificial intelligence company in Beijing. This company specializes in cutting-edge AI research and applications, providing me with a vast stage to showcase my talents. After joining the company, I actively participated in the research and development of several projects. Notably, in a study on the relationship between footprints and shoeprint measurements, I applied convolutional neural networks to estimate height. I was also responsible for a project involving the detection of daily consumer goods in vending machines. For this, I developed a YOLOv3 model which is capable of multi-object detection for 20 different products. In these projects, I leveraged the innovative thinking cultivated during my academic research to create several market-competitive intelligent system solutions for the company.

New Challenges and Prospects

In 2021, I decided to embrace a new challenge by relocating to Guangzhou and joining CloudWalk Technology, a prestigious company in the AI field. This company focuses on technological innovation in areas such as intelligent transportation and smart cities, with a corporate culture that emphasizes innovation and teamwork, which aligns perfectly with my personal pursuits. I am eager to contribute my expertise to developing intelligent solutions for modern urban transportation challenges. At CloudWalk, I primarily focused on research involving LLMs, a deep learning technology for natural language processing. LLMs represent a significant breakthrough in AI, enabling machines to better understand and generate human language. In my first year with the company, I led a team to transform this technology into practical solutions, and developed a language model named TransGPT. Designed specifically for the transportation industry, this model leverages big data to analyze traffic flow and predict congestion. By analyzing data and continuously optimizing the model, we achieved precise traffic flow predictions and intelligent scheduling. TransGPT provided scientific support for traffic management in multiple cities and addressed key challenges in urban transportation.

I also participated in a collaborative project with Huawei, focusing on integrating the computational requirements of LLMs with Huawei's Ascend platform. Ascend platform is an AI computing platform designed to provide powerful computational support for AI applications. Working closely with the Huawei team, we explored how to optimize LLMs through quantization techniques, enabling efficient performance on the Ascend platform. In this process, I utilized my expertise in machine learning and algorithm optimization, contributing significantly to the technological advancement of the Ascend platform. This collaboration not only further strengthened CloudWalk's technological advantages in intelligent transportation but also earned me greater recognition within the company and the broader industry. My research results provided new technological support for the intelligent development of the transportation sector while opening new directions for the scalability of LLMs in practical applications.

I have constantly reflected on the relationship between technology and human life. I not only focus on how technology can be applied across various industries but also aspire to ensure it genuinely serves society and benefits humanity. I firmly believe that advancements in AI are not merely technical breakthroughs. They have the potential to profoundly impact social operations, urban management, and human lifestyles. This conviction has driven me to center my work on intelligent transportation and smart city research, aiming to alleviate traffic congestion, reduce carbon emissions, and enhance urban efficiency through the power of AI.

I understand that my achievements are closely tied to my educational experience at Beihang University. That period laid a solid foundation in engineering, taught me how to conduct interdisciplinary research, and, most importantly, helped me realize that the essence of academia goes beyond solving problems—it lies in broadening perspectives and driving societal progress. I often reminisce about my time at Beihang University, especially the moments I shared with my supervisor, Professor Yuan. He not only imparted professional knowledge but also shaped me into a responsible researcher, teaching me to integrate theory with practice to create value for society. I also recognize that my success is not solely the result of my own efforts but the outcome of the selfless support and guidance of my mentors and friends. Therefore, I maintain an open mindset in my work, readily accepting others' opinions and respecting everyone I collaborate with. At the same time, I strive to share my knowledge and experiences with younger individuals, hoping to help them avoid detours and find success sooner.

As a senior AI researcher, the field's rapid advancements and increasing competition make my life both challenging and full of opportunities. However, I remain humble and pragmatic, no matter how much pressure I face. I sustain my boundless enthusiasm for technology and my patience in solving problems, firmly believing that hard work will eventually pay off. While my work often keeps me on edge, my life is vibrant and fulfilling. I have developed a deep appreciation for Chinese cuisine, constantly exploring different regional specialties. From Beijing's Zhajiang noodles to Guangzhou's dim sum, from Sichuan's spicy hot pot to Northeastern China's pickled cabbage stew, these dishes have allowed me to experience the unique charm of China's diverse regions.

If I were to summarize my story with a few keywords, they would be *struggle* and *achievement*—a narrative best embodied by an international student who, through relentless effort, found his place in the vast land of China and then leveraged the power of technology to promote social development and enhance people's quality of life. Whether in study or work, I have always maintained a passion for technology, enthusiasm for life, and unwavering confidence in the future. Today, I stand at the forefront of AI research and development, dedicated to further optimizing and applying LLMs. Looking ahead, I am full of hope, and I firmly believe that with the continuous progress of technology, AI will demonstrate its importance in more and more fields. I am eager to further promote the application of AI technology in various industries, especially in intelligent transportation, smart cities, and other areas, helping more cities achieve intelligent management, bringing substantial improvements to people's lives, and contributing my part to the development of global intelligence. At the same time, I also look forward to continuing to collaborate with top scholars and companies worldwide in my future work to jointly drive technological progress.

My story is about unremitting dream pursuit. I came to China from Peru, overcame numerous cultural and language barriers, climbed the peaks of academia, and now find myself in a career filled with challenges and opportunities. Whether it was in the academic research or my career, I have always maintained a rigorous attitude and fearless spirit, constantly embracing new challenges and surpassing myself. My story is far from over, no matter how rough the road ahead may be, I will press on with determination, striving for a bright and promising future.

Message from the Supervisor

During Edwin's postgraduate studies, the rise of 3D vision and AI presented a great opportunity. He made remarkable achievements by applying Kinect to yoga teaching. I am extremely proud of his innovative spirit. His performance in applying AI algorithms in this industry is outstanding. He has not only grasped complex theories but also transformed them into practical solutions, driving innovation and progress.

His study at Beihang University was filled with dedication and diligence. This is just the beginning. The knowledge and skills he has acquired are his tools to explore the world. I hope he can march forward with full confidence, continuously explore the vast potential of AI and make a greater impact on the global stage. May his journey be filled with success and gain!

Introduction to the Supervisor

Peijiang Yuan is an associate professor and master's supervisor at the School of Mechanical Engineering and Automation, Beihang University. He has published more than 50 papers in renowned domestic and international journals and at conferences, among which more than 30 are indexed by SCI, EI, ISTP. He has also undertaken a number of interdisciplinary research projects related to intelligent control and Embodied AI robots. He participated in the teaching reform project Bilingual Teaching of Electromechanical Control Engineering Technology. In addition, he actively participated in the application for national key projects, including the application for Major Programs of the National Natural Science Foundation of China, the 973 Program and so on. He once served as an associate editor on the conference committees of ICRA 2011 and IROS 2011, as the session chair of WCICA 2010, as the session chair of ICIEA 2014, as an editorial board member of *IJARS* (an SCI journal), as the secretary of the 863 Advanced Manufacturing Expert Group.

Love Story at Beihang
University

07

在北航收获爱情

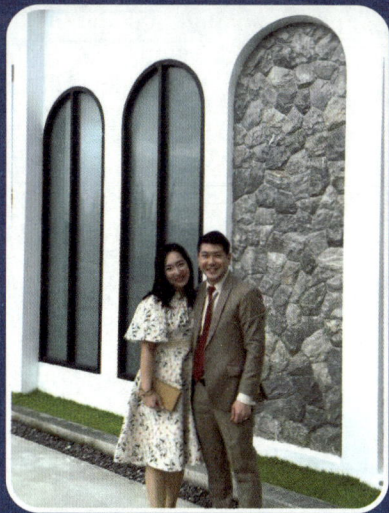

伟波（右）和刘芝清合影

伟　波、刘芝清

　　伟波（Wipot）、刘芝清（Pipassa）都来自泰国。谈到伟波，不止一个老师认为他是那届北航汉语班最优秀的学生。伟波与刘芝清两人在北航相识，当时他们都忙于学习，没有确立恋爱关系，回泰国后共同语言多了起来，渐渐成为情侣，继而组成了小家庭。他们因北航而燃起的爱情故事深刻诠释了"Do not disturb love until it is ready"这句话。

　　Wipot and Pipassa, both from Thailand, share a special bond with Beihang University. When it comes to Wipot, more than one teacher believes that he was the most outstanding student in the Chinese class of Beihang University that year. During their time at the university, they put their focus on their studies, and they were not a couple yet. However, their shared experiences at Beihang University laid the foundation for their connection, which later blossomed into love after they returned to Thailand. Their love story ignited by Beihang University perfectly interpreted the saying "Do not disturb love until it is ready."

伟波：来中国前我在泰国学习的是日语，一年后日语达到了中级，学习过程开始出现汉字。汉字非常难记，我感觉有点儿学不下去了。但我想既然有汉字要不就先学汉语吧，于是 2008 年左右，我开始在泰国补习班学习汉语。一开始学习汉语是为了记住日语汉字，然后去日本留学。学习了一年左右，我逐渐发现，原来汉语也非常有意思，虽然汉字很难记，但是汉语的语法很奇妙。不同于泰国老师教英语的方式，我的第一个汉语老师采用沉浸式教汉语，这使我对汉语学习产生浓厚兴趣，并考虑来中国留学。促使我放弃日本来中国留学的另一个原因是学费。我是自费留学，如果去日本，只够学习一年，但是到中国可能可以学两年。基于这两个原因，我与中国的缘分就这么开始了。中介最开始向我推荐了成都，但我觉得北京是首都，会下雪，名胜古迹也更多，在北京可以边学习边旅游，就这样我来到了北航。

刘芝清：我大学毕业后与同学一起来到北航。我选择北航是因为那时北航的泰国学生相对来说不多，我不想到了国外还扎在一起说泰语。我和伟波是泰国人中比较早选择到中国留学的一批人。我们觉得我们的眼光独特，认定了汉语将来一定会大有前途，所以毅然决然地来到了异国。我在北航只读了一年的汉语，没有攻读专业学位。而且来北航时，我的汉语是从中级开始

刘芝清（一排左一）和同学们在课堂

学习的。一年后回国，凭借着北航锻炼出来的良好汉语水平，我在泰国亚洲航空公司谋到了职位。在平时的工作中，我在北航所学的汉语发挥了极大的作用。在航空公司飞往中国各大城市的国际航线中，面对中国的顾客，我的所学有了用武之地。毕业近十年来，来泰国旅游的中国游客人数稳定，去中国旅游的泰国游客也日渐增多。中国地大物博，旅游资源丰富，中泰两国又互免签证，为双方的国民带来了极大的便利。在日常的工作中，因为我在北航留过学，深入地了解过中国的文化，所以除了语言沟通，也能为中国人提供更优质的服务，同时还能作为中泰两国的文化使者，传播双方的友谊与善意。

朱老师（伟波的汉语老师）： 伟波在 2009 年 9 月打破"金饭碗"，从泰国一家银行辞职来到北航汉语班学习，给汉语班的所有老师留下了非常深刻的印象。他出勤良好，脚踏实地，从初级读到高级，给所有学生树立了榜样。研究生学习期间，他依然不放松语言学习，在专业课之余坚持在汉语班上课。他做什么事情都一丝不苟，很多老师多年后提起伟波依然赞不绝口。

伟波： 我研究生期间读的是工商管理专业。回国成家立业后，考虑到刘芝清需要经常出差，与朝九晚五的生活比起来，可能在自己家的公司工作，时间更有弹性，更自由些，于是我接手了家族生意。我做生意的原材料都来自中国。近年来，设备也越来越多从中国进口。与欧洲国家相比，中国的设备质量良好，但价格仅为欧洲国家的一半，是我们最优的选择。我也把自己在北航学习的工商管理的专业知识用到了家族企业管理中，在北航的所学完全致力于如今所为。

刘芝清： 2024 年 7 月，亚洲航空公司开通曼谷至北京的航线，我们夫妻二人就确定了返回北京看望母校的行程。回泰国快十年了，我们经常会回忆在北京的生活，而且同学们一起聊天时，也经常聊起想回学校看看。这已经变成了每一个在北航学习过的国际学生都向往的事。7 月，我们带着五岁多的儿子专程回到了母校，看了学校，见了老师和以前的朋友。与十年前相比，我们感受到的最大变化是学校出现了很多新建筑，包括新宿舍楼、北区食堂等，新建筑比以前更雄伟、更壮观、更漂亮、更便捷。让我们感到非常欣慰的是，我们的儿子非常喜欢北京航空航天博物馆，对各种飞机兴趣盎然，对飞机模型爱不释手。

　　我至今仍然清晰地记得每天上学必经的那条从大运村到国际学院的道

路，春日的鸟鸣，夏日的浓荫，秋日的金黄落叶，冬日的瑟瑟寒风与皑皑白雪绘成一幅幅美丽的画面。我当年最爱吃操场旁边摊上的鸡蛋灌饼，若灌饼里放辣椒，我吃了就会长痘，所以我的室友（泰国学生黄君薇）就可以从我脸上有没有长痘准确地判断我是否偷着去买了鸡蛋灌饼吃。这次回北京，我带儿子去品尝的美食是北京烤鸭，而我则第一天就扑向了我最思念的鸡蛋灌饼。谈及学校和老师们，我们对汉语班的任课老师印象深刻，老师们的教学方法使我们受益匪浅。

一家三口

伟波： 我在北航读了两年汉语班，又读了三年研究生。因为在北航待了五年多，我被后来的泰国学生戏称为"北航爷爷"。也正是因为读研究生，我赶上了第一届北航国际文化节。在第一届国际文化节上，我组织泰国学生进行了泰拳表演，场面十分震撼。我也与其他泰国学生结下了深厚的友谊，

第一届北航国际文化节

至今我们仍然常常见面，一起做饭，一起回味在北航的生活。

岁月如梭，青春如歌。我们在北航的日子，虽然忙碌，却也充满了无尽的乐趣。在那段青葱岁月里，我们不仅学会了知识，更学会了如何面对困难，如何在逆境中坚持自己的梦想。我们结识了志同道合的朋友，遇到了启迪智慧的老师，更在无数次的探索与尝试中，逐渐明确了自己的人生方向。北航的每一个角落，都留下了我们青春的足迹，每一片树叶，都见证了我们的成长与蜕变。

朱老师：如今，伟波与刘芝清已经携手走过了多个春秋，他们的小家庭温馨而幸福。虽然远隔千里，但他们心中对北航的思念与感激却从未减退。每当回忆起在北航的点点滴滴，他们的脸上总会洋溢出幸福的笑容。未来的日子里，无论他们身处何方，无论面临怎样的困难与挑战，相信他们都会怀揣着在北航收获的勇气与智慧，继续前行，在各自的领域里发光发热。

导师寄语

伟波是来自泰国的 2011 级硕士生，2014 年毕业，他在求学期间给我留下了深刻的印象。

记得第一次见面是在我的办公室，推门进来的是一位帅气的小伙子，他非常谦逊有礼貌，谈吐文雅。而且没想到他的汉语那么好，一般和国际学生沟通我都是说英语，而我们俩几句寒暄过后就直接用汉语交流，基本上没什么障碍，这给了我一个惊喜。之后，在我们每一次的专业讨论中，他都能做到认真准备，详细阅读布置的文献，并积极思考，提出问题，尤其在撰写学位论文的过程中注重理论与实际相结合，表现出了很强的分析和研究问题的能力。

一晃伟波毕业已经十多年了，看着他接掌家族企业，有了幸福的小家庭，真为他高兴。祝他在今后的日子里工作顺利、事业有成，企业兴旺发达，家庭幸福！有空闲时间的话多回北航看看！

导师简介

杨梅英，北航经济管理学院教授，博士生导师。研究方向为企业管理理论与应用、技术经济分析。为本科生讲授微观经济学，为研究生讲授微观经济理论，同时为工商管理硕士（MBA）讲授管理经济学，深受学生的喜爱与认可。近年来主持完成多项国家级、省部级科研课题以及企业咨询项目的研究，如国家自然科学基金重点项目的子课题"中国制造业企业市场营销对国际竞争力影响的研究"、国家自然科学基金项目"超竞争环境下企业的合作竞争模式研究"、航空科学基金项目"全要素生产率与航空工业经济增长"等。

Wipot: Before coming to China, I studied Japanese in Thailand. Upon attaining an intermediate level in Japanese through a year of study, I began encountering kanji (Chinese) characters, which were extremely difficult to remember. I felt somewhat discouraged. But I thought, since there were Chinese characters, I might as well start learning Chinese first. Around 2008, I began learning Chinese in Thailand, with the initial intention of mastering Japanese kanji through Chinese and studying in Japan in the future. But to my surprise, I found Chinese quite fascinating. While the characters were still challenging, the grammar and teaching methods intrigued me, particularly the immersive style my first teacher used, which was very different from how English was taught in Thailand, sparking my deep interest in learning Chinese. Another reason why I chose China instead of Japan for study was the cost of tuition. I was fully self-funded, and the money I had would only cover one year of study in Japan, whereas it might suffice for two years in China. Due to both reasons, my fate with China was sowed. The agency initially recommended Chengdu to me, but I chose Beijing since it is the capital. Furthermore, Beijing snows in winter and has more famous historical places, allowing me to study knowledge and culture simultaneously. This is how my journey at Beihang University began.

Pipassa: I came to Beihang University with my classmate after graduating from university. I chose Beihang University because there weren't many Thai students there at that time, and I wanted to avoid sticking to speaking Thai abroad. Wipot and I were among the Thai students who chose to study in China in the early times. We believe that the Chinese would have a bright future, and coming to China should be the right decision. At Beihang University, I studied Chinese for a year, starting from the intermediate level, but didn't pursue a degree. After returning to Thailand one year later, I found a job at Thai AirAsia thanks to the excellent Chinese language skills I acquired at Beihang University. On international flights to major cities in China, my knowledge and skills play an important role when serving Chinese customers. In the nearly ten years since my graduation, the number of Chinese tourists traveling to Thailand has remained stable, while the number of Thai tourists visiting China has gradually increased a lot. China has a vast territory and abundant resources, as well as rich tourist attractions. In addition, the mutual visa exemption between China and Thailand has brought great convenience to people of both countries. In my daily work, besides my language skills, the cultural insights I gained at Beihang University enable me to provide better services to Chinese people, and help me serve as a cultural ambassador, promoting mutual understanding and friendship between China and Thailand.

Teacher Zhu (Wipot's Chinese Teacher): In September 2009, Wipot broke his "golden bowl". He resigned from a bank in Thailand and came to study Chinese at Beihang University, leaving a deep impression on all the teachers. He hardly ever missed classes. He was diligent and studied from beginner to advanced levels, setting a good example for all international students. Even during his master's studies in business administration, he continued taking language classes and maintained his commitment to learning. He was meticulous in everything, and many of the Chinese teachers still speak highly of him to this day.

Wipot: After completing my MBA at Beihang University, I returned to Thailand and got married. My wife needs to travel frequently from country to country. Since running our family company offered flexibility and a better work-life balance, I joined the family business. Almost all the raw materials for my business come from China. In recent years, we have increasingly imported equipment from China. Compared to European imports, Chinese equipment provides better quality at half the price, making it our optimal choice. I have applied the MBA knowledge I learned to the management of our family business, fully dedicating what I learned at Beihang University to what I do now.

Pipassa: When the airline launched its Bangkok-Beijing route in July 2024, my husband and I immediately decided to return to Beijing to visit our alma mater. It has been nearly a decade since we left, but we often chat about the life at Beihang University. When we chatted with our classmates, we knew that revisiting the university is something that every international student who has studied at Beihang University wants to do. In July, we returned to our alma mater with our five-year-old son, visiting the school, meeting with teachers, and seeing old friends. Compared to ten years ago, the biggest change we noticed was the new buildings, such as the new dormitories and the north district canteen, which are more magnificent, spectacular, and convenient. We were happy to see that our son loved the Beijing Aeronautics and Astronautics Museum very much, showing great interest in various airplanes, and couldn't bear to part with the airplane models.

I still remember the path we took every day from Dayuncun student apartment to the International School. The cheerful chirping of birds in spring, the dense shade of summer, the golden leaves of autumn, and the biting winter winds accompanied by snow created a series of beautiful scenes. What is the most impressive to me is the egg-filled pancakes, my favorite snack sold at the stall by the playground. Chili inside the pancake often caused acne. My roommate, Junwei Huang, another student from Thailand, could accurately tell whether I had secretly indulged in one just by looking at my face. This time, during my visit to Beijing, I treated my son to Peking duck, but on my very first day, I couldn't wait and directly ran to the egg-filled pancake because I had missed it so much. We have a deep impression of the Chinese teachers. Their teaching methods have benefited us a lot.

Wipot: After completing two years of Chinese studies, I continued with three years of postgraduate studies. Since I was at Beihang University for more than five years, I was nicknamed "Grandpa at Beihang University" by newer Thai students. During my postgraduate years, I attended Beihang University's first International Cultural Festival, where I organized Thai students to give a Muay Thai performance. The scene was breathtaking, and it was during this event that I forged deep and lasting friendships with other Thai students. To this day, we still often meet and cook together, missing our days at Beihang University.

Time flies, and youth is like a song. Our days at Beihang University were busy, but they were also filled with endless joy. In those golden years, we not only gained knowledge but also learned how to face difficulties and persist in our dreams amidst adversity. At Beihang University, we made good friends, encountered inspiring teachers, and, through countless explorations and practices, gradually clarified our life ambitions. Every corner of Beihang University holds traces of our youth, and every leaf witnesses our growth and transformation.

Teacher Zhu: Today, Wipot and Pipassa have joined hands for many years, building a warm and happy family. Although they no longer live in China, their longing and gratitude for Beihang University remain as strong as ever. Their faces light up with joyful smiles whenever they reminisce about their time at Beihang University. In the days ahead, no matter where they will be or what challenges and difficulties they may face, they will carry the courage and wisdom they gained at Beihang University, continuing to move forward and shine brightly in their respective fields.

Message from the Supervisor

Wipot is a student from Thailand. He began his master's study in 2011 and graduated in 2014. He left a deep impression on me.

I still remember our first meeting in my office. A handsome young man with elegant speech entered, extremely humble and polite. To my surprise, his Chinese was unexpectedly good. Usually, I communicate with international students in English, but after a few pleasantries, we switched to Chinese without any barriers, which was a pleasant surprise. In every research discussion, he was well-prepared, having read the assigned literature thoroughly, and actively thought and raised questions. In his thesis research, he focused on combining theory with practice, demonstrating strong analytical and research skills.

It has been more than ten years since Wipot graduated. I am thrilled that he has taken over the family business and has a happy family. I wish him smooth work, a successful career, prosperity in his enterprise, and happiness in his family in the days to come. If he has spare time, I hope he comes back to visit alma mater often!

Introduction to the Supervisor

Meiying Yang is a professor and doctoral supervisor at the School of Economics and Management, Beihang University. Her research directions are enterprise management theory and application, technical and economic analysis. She teaches the course Microeconomics to undergraduate students, the course Microeconomic Theory to postgraduate students, and the course Managerial Economics to MBA students. She is deeply loved and recognized by students. In recent years, she has completed the research of a number of national, provincial and ministerial-level scientific research projects as well as enterprise consulting projects, such as Research on the Impact of Marketing of Chinese Manufacturing Enterprises on Their International Competitiveness, the sub-project supported by the Key Program of the National Natural Science Foundation of China; and Research on the Cooperative Competition Model of Enterprises in a Hypercompetitive Environment, the project supported by the National Natural Science Foundation of China; Total Factor Productivity and the Economic Growth of the Aviation Industry, the project of the Aeronautical Science Foundation.

From "Nihao" to Technical Expert: My Journey at Beihang University

08

从"你好"到技术专家：我的北航之路

伊 万

　　伊万（Iván），来自哥伦比亚。他在北航演绎了一个执着的追梦故事。伊万怀着对计算机科学的热爱和对中国信息产业的憧憬，选择攻读计算机专业。2016年本科毕业之际，他满怀在信息领域继续深入钻研的期望，毅然选择在北航继续攻读硕士学位，师从计算机学院李舟军教授。伊万在学术方面持续奋进，深入研究专业知识，踊跃参加专业领域的校内外技术实践活动和学术交流会议，与不同文化背景、不同学术层次的专业人士分享、交流学科前沿知识，不断拓宽自己的专业视野和知识储备。2019年，伊万完成了他的学业，同时也开启了人生崭新的征程，怀着对计算机专业的无限热爱和坚定信念，他加入一家大型互联网企业，全身心投入到信息领域工作中，致力于为信息技术的发展贡献自己的力量。

　　Iván, from Colombia, embarked on an unforgettable journey of chasing his dream at Beihang University. Driven by his passion for computer science and China's information industry, Iván chose to major in computer science. When he graduated from the undergraduate program in 2016, with the expectation of continuing in-depth study and further education in the field of information technology, he resolutely chose to continue his master's degree at Beihang University, under the supervision of Professor Zhoujun Li in the School of Computer Science. Iván made good efforts in academics, studying professional knowledge, and actively participated in technical practice activities and academic conferences in and outside campus, sharing and exchanging cutting-edge knowledge with professionals from different cultural backgrounds and academic levels, which constantly broadened his professional horizon and knowledge. In 2019, Iván completed his study, starting a new journey in his life. Falling in love with and insisting on the belief in information technology, he joined a big Internet enterprise, devoting himself wholeheartedly to the field of information technology research and committed to contributing his strength to the development of this field.

回首我在北航的求学岁月，那是一段充满挑战、机遇并且不断提升自我的难忘旅途。从本科阶段学习计算机工程，再到研究生阶段投身于信息技术研究，每一天我都在不断学习与成长。在母校的学习生活中，我不仅接触到了最前沿的学科与技术知识，还通过参与项目实践、跨文化交流，以及应对语言挑战，获得了许多宝贵的经验。

命运转折点：从语言学习到学术深造

2008 年对我来说是一个具有特殊意义的年份，我原本计划来中国学习一年的汉语，之后返回我的国家完成本科课程。刚抵达中国时，北京刚好在举办世界瞩目的奥运会，大街小巷都装点着奥运元素，整个城市充满了浓郁的奥运氛围。尽管四周热闹无比，我却连最简单的"你好"都不会说。这给初来乍到的我当头一击，每一次想要与人交流，都只能用手势比画加几个简单的英语单词，内心的窘迫和无助感油然而生。与此同时，我深深被中国的文化、历史以及科技资源所吸引。当我漫步在北京古老的胡同里，看到那些传统的四合院建筑时，仿佛穿越时空，感受到历史的厚重与沉淀。纵观中国近几十年的飞速发展，我感受到这个国家有着无限的可能性，特别是在学术研究和技术创新方面，处处充满机遇，这对于我后续的学习探索将是一个重要的助力。

时光流转，我逐渐适应了中国的生活，并且发现这里不仅是学习语言的好地方，也是开展学术研究的理想之地。于是，我开始重新思考自己未来的发展方向，并且下定决心要继续在中国深造。就在这个时候，我留意到北

伊万（二排右三）与预科班同学合影

航推出的预科项目，这个项目的课程设置非常合理且丰富。上午安排汉语课程，提高我的汉语水平，为我在中国的学习和生活奠定更好的语言基础。下午教授数学、化学和物理等科目，这些科目都是学术研究重要的基础学科。对于我来说，这无疑是一个千载难逢的机会。所以，我毫不犹豫地报名参加了这个项目，也正是从做出这个决定的那一刻起，我便正式开启了自己在北航的求学征程。

语言的挑战：从西班牙语到汉语的转换

对我来说，语言始终是一个挑战。我的母语是西班牙语，学习汉语的过程让我深刻感受到两种语言的巨大差异。西班牙语声调单一，运用字母表，没有复杂的发音变化，而汉语却完全不同，它有四个声调，发音注重声调和音节的清晰度，并且发音中有许多类似的音，例如"sh""zh""ch""c"和"z"，这对我是一项极大的考验。当时的我仿佛置身于一个充满陌生声音的迷宫之中，耳朵根本没有为辨别这些微妙且复杂的发音做好准备。每一个发音都像是一个独特的密码，有着细微而又关键的差别，而我却如同一个没有掌握密码规则的探索者，茫然不知所措。

记得有一回，在数据库课程课间休息的时候，郎波老师让大家把作业放到她的桌子上。当时的我，完全不知道还有作业要交，于是扭头问同桌威尔逊："咱们有作业吗？"他一脸惊讶地看着我，回答道："当然，老师两天前就布置了关于 X 图的作业了。"听到这话，我又惊又惑，因为我压根就没听到这项作业的要求啊。后来我才发现，在那堂课上，可能是由于语言障碍，我没能彻底理解老师的指示。幸运的是，郎老师特别理解我的难处，允许我晚些时候再补交作业。这次经历让我意识到自己在语言理解上还有很多需要提升的地方，同时也让我深刻明白在学习的时候集中注意力是多么重要的一件事。

尽管如此，我始终坚信学习语言就像跑一场马拉松，需要耐心和持续的努力。我反复提醒自己"这不是一场百米冲刺赛跑，而是一场持久的马拉松"。怀着这种信念，我每天都投入大量时间与精力去练习发音、听力和阅读。在学习汉语的道路上，我经历了无数的困难，发音不准确、用词不恰当，都像是前进路上的绊脚石。但是，我没有被这些困难吓倒，无论是简单的日常词汇还是复杂的学术用语，我都反复练习，斟酌恰当的用词。就这样，经过长时间的努力，我终于能够比较流利地使用汉语与老师和同学们进行交流。虽然我的汉语还不是那么完美，在一些生僻字的读音上偶尔还会出错，在一些正式、书面化的表达上还不够精准，但是我已经可以应对大学课程中的各种交流需求了。在课堂上，我可以清晰地回答老师的问题；在日常生活中，我能够自如地和中国同学聊天，不再因为语言的障碍而感到困扰。

技术实践：从课堂学习到个人项目的提升

除了应对语言上的挑战外，课程学习也是我在北航的重要组成部分。在此，我特别感激学校提供的实践机会，让我得以突破书本知识的局限，通过动手操作获得实践经验。在我的本科阶段，我有幸参与了许多技术实践课程，例如学习如何使用激光切割机来制造零件，这让我感受到现代先进技术在零件制造方面的高效与精准；我还参与了金属铸造模具的制作，深入了解模具制作的各个环节以及其中所蕴含的工程学原理；操作车床也是我学习内容的一部分，我掌握了车床的基本操作方法以及如何根据不同的需求加工出符合要求的工件。这些技术实践活动对我而言意义非凡，一方面，它们锻炼了我的动手能力，让我能够熟练地操作各种工具和设备；另一方面，这些实践活动让我对工程学的基础原理有了更为透彻的理解。

有一个项目给我留下了极为深刻的印象。这个项目的内容是拆卸并重新组装一辆自行车。在这之前，我没有任何机械操作的经验。不过，通过团队成员之间的协作，加上一步一步地摸索学习，我最终还是成功地掌握了这项技能。每次完成一个项目后，我和同学们都会感到精疲力竭。好几次项目结束，我们累得浑身无力，回到宿舍倒在床上就呼呼大睡，但心中充满了强烈的成就感。这些实践经历使我认识到，工程学并非仅仅局限于理论上的推导演绎，更为关键的，是要懂得在实际操作当中应用理论解决各种各样的问题。

在课外实践中，我也努力提高自身的技能水平。学校距离中关村很近，我经常到那里采购硬件设备。我曾经买过一台树莓派，并搭配了各种模块进行实验。我运用它构建了小型网络工具进行数据传输和网络监控。这使我对硬件和软件的结合有了更好的理解，并且为我研究生阶段撰写有关移动自组织网络（MANET）方面的论文提供了非常实用的帮助。除此之外，我还自主开发了一款基于 Linux 操作系统的远程管理工具，这个项目不仅加深了我对操作系统的理解，还提升了我的网络管理能力。

上述这些项目让我在实际操作中灵活运用课堂所学，并为我后续的学术研究和职业发展打下坚实的基础。

跨文化交流：从学生会到国际舞台

除了学术能力的成长，跨文化交流能力的提升也是不可忽视的一部分。我有幸成为国际学院学生会的一员，这一身份让我获得了与来自五湖四海的同学进行互动的宝贵机会。在与不同国家的同学的交往过程中，我深切地感受到跨文化交流的独特魅力，对不同的文化背景有了更为深入的理解，并且发自内心地尊重这种多元性。例如，在与欧洲同学合作项目时，我了解到他们对于时间管理的严谨态度以及在团队讨论中直抒己见的沟通风格；而与亚洲不同国家的同学相处时，又能感受到相似文化根源下的细微差别，比如对待集体荣誉时，不同人有着不同的表达方式等。

参加学生会活动

我还记得有一回，学生会举办了一场有关国家节日的活动。在这次活动里，我深入了解了马来西亚、印度尼西亚等国家的文化传统，同时，我也向他们介绍了西班牙语国家的一些文化传统与习俗。这些文化交流活动让我沉浸式学习其他国家文化的同时，也能传播自己国家的文化。我认为这样的活动意义非凡，不仅展现了世界文化的多样性，也让我学会如何与他人和谐合作，明白建立友谊和合作的重要基础是尊重和理解。这类跨文化交流活动一直以来深受学生们的欢迎。

在分享文化的同时，我在学习期间也多次获得了在国际舞台上展示专业知识的机会。作为信息领域的研究者，我曾多次受邀在国际会议上发表演讲。记得在韩国的一次大会上，我主讲的课题吸引了多个国家的听众，很多人都对这个课题表现出浓厚的兴趣。在西班牙的一次会议中，我就量子密码学的前沿发展进行了演讲，并与在场来自世界各地的专家进行深入交流。这些学术交流，一方面，极大地丰富了我的知识储备，让我接触到不同国家在信息领域的研究成果和思路；另一方面，也使我更加坚定了在信息领域深入钻研的决心，我深知这个领域还有许多未知等待我去探索，还有许多挑战需要我去应对。

校友纽带：北航的影响力

在与人们交流互动的时候，别人只要知道我能用汉语进行沟通，就会好奇地问我是在哪所大学就读的，而每当我回答"我来自北航"的时候，大家几乎毫无例外地称赞北航是一所相当不错的大学。有时候，我还会碰到北航的校友。这种关系和联结往往能够打开新的机会之门，无论是在职业发展上，还是在专业合作中，这种归属感以及带来的机遇总是让我感到幸运和自豪。

随着中国国际化步伐的不断加快，加上北航一直以来积极地与世界各国开展广泛的交流与合作，我相信未来会有越来越多优秀的国际学生加入北航大家庭。他们也将像我一样，通过留学北航，不断积累学科知识，拓宽学术视野，提升学术能力，同时深入体验中

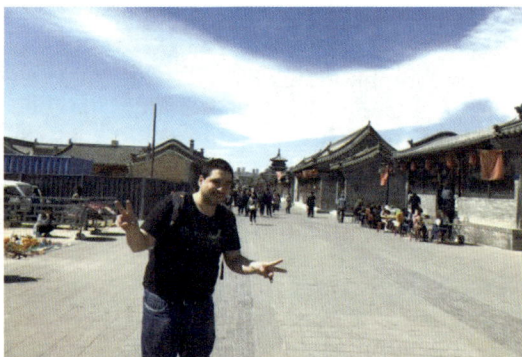

伊万在中国

华文化的魅力，与不同文化背景的同学建立深厚的友谊，促进多元文化的交流与融合，继而在北航这个大舞台上，充分施展个人所长，并把在中国学到的知识和理念运用到自己国家的建设和发展之中。

Reflecting on my years of study at Beihang University, I found it to be an unforgettable journey filled with challenges, opportunities, and continuous self-improvement. From an undergraduate student studying computer engineering to a graduate student diving into information technology research, my journey at Beihang University was a continuous progression of learning, growth and professional development. During my time there, I got the chance to be exposed to cutting-edge academic and technological knowledge. Meanwhile, I accumulated valuable experiences through project participation, cross-cultural exchanges, and overcoming language barriers.

Turning Point: From Language Learning to Academic Pursuit

2008 was a special year for me, as I had planned to spend one year in China studying Chinese and then return to my home country to complete my undergraduate studies. When I first arrived, Beijing was hosting the highly anticipated Olympic Games. The streets were adorned with Olympic decorations, and the city was alive with the vibrant atmosphere of the event. Despite the lively surroundings, I quickly realized that I couldn't even say the simplest "Nihao" (hello) in Chinese. This hit me hard. Every attempt to communicate often ended with gestures and a few English words, leaving me feeling embarrassed and helpless. At the same time, I was deeply captivated by China's culture, history, and technological resources. While strolling through Beijing's ancient Hutong and marveling at the traditional courtyard houses, I was overwhelmed by a sense of traveling through time and space, deeply immersing myself in the richness of history. Taking a broad view of China's rapid development over the past few decades, I sensed the immense potential of this nation, particularly in academic research and technological innovation. I realized that staying in China would be beneficial for my future study and exploration.

As time passed, I gradually adapted to the life in China and discovered that it was not only an excellent place to learn the language but also an ideal environment for academic pursuits. I began to rethink my future direction and resolved to continue my studies in China. It was at this time that I learned about Beihang University's preparatory program for international students, which offered a well-structured and comprehensive curriculum. I took Chinese classes in the morning to improve my language skills and build a solid foundation for life and study in China, followed by mathematics, chemistry, and physics classes in the afternoon, which were essential for academic research. For me, this was a golden opportunity. Without hesitation, I decided to enroll in the program, marking the beginning of my academic journey at Beihang University. From the moment I made that decision, I embarked on a path that would shape my future profoundly.

Language Challenge: The conversion from Spanish to Chinese

For me, language has always been a challenge. As a native Spanish speaker, learning Chinese made me acutely aware of the vast differences between the two languages. Spanish uses a straightforward alphabet and lacks tonal variations. Chinese, on the other hand, features four tones, requires precision in syllables and pronunciation, and includes many similar sounds such as "sh", "zh", "ch", "c" and "z". This presented a tremendous challenge for me. I vividly remember feeling trapped in a labyrinth of unfamiliar sounds, where my ears were unprepared to discern these subtle, intricate differences. Every sound seemed like a unique code with slight but critical distinctions, and I was an explorer without the key to unlocking the rules of these codes, feeling lost and bewildered.

One memorable incident occurred during a Database class. During a break, our teacher, Ms. Bo Lang, asked everyone to submit their assignments on her desk. I was completely unaware of any assignment and turned to my deskmate, Wilson, to ask, "Do we have homework?" He looked at me, astonished, and replied, "Of course. The teacher assigned a task on X-diagrams two days ago." I was both surprised and confused, realizing I had completely missed the assignment instructions. Later, I realized that due to my difficulty in understanding the language, I hadn't fully grasped the teacher's directions during that lesson. Thankfully, Ms. Lang fully understood my situation and allowed me to submit the homework later this time. This experience served as a wake-up call, reminding me not only of how much I still needed to improve my language comprehension but also of the importance of staying focused and attentive during lessons.

Despite these difficulties, I firmly believed that learning a language was like running a marathon, as it required patience and sustained effort. I constantly reminded myself, "This isn't a sprint. It's a marathon." With this mindset, I focused my time, thought and energy on practicing pronunciation, listening, and reading in Chinese. The journey was filled with countless challenges. Every mispronunciation or inappropriate word choice seemed like a stumbling block. However, I was not deterred by these setbacks. Instead, I chose to practice repeatedly and carefully refine my word usage, from simple daily vocabulary to complex academic terminology. After a long period of hard work, I reached a level where I could communicate relatively fluently with my teachers and classmates in Chinese. Though my Chinese is still not perfect, for instance, I occasionally mispronounce obscure characters or struggle with formal and written expressions. But it has become sufficient for handling university coursework and day-to-day communication. In class, I could answer teachers' questions clearly, and in daily life, I could chat smoothly with my Chinese classmates without being hindered by language barriers.

Technical Practice: Advance from Classroom Learning to Personal Projects

Beyond language challenges, coursework formed a vital part of my study here. I am especially grateful for the opportunities provided by the university, which allowed me to go beyond textbooks and gain practical experience through hands-on applications. During my undergraduate years, I participated in various technical practice courses. For instance, I learned how to use a laser cutter to manufacture parts, which demonstrated the efficiency and precision of modern technology in part fabrication. I also took part in a metal casting mold-making course, which gave me an in-depth understanding of the stages involved in mold production and the engineering principles embedded in them. Additionally, I acquired basic skills in operating a lathe, enabling me to process workpieces according to specific requirements. These technical practices were invaluable to me. On the one hand, they significantly enhanced my practical skills, enabling me to operate various tools and machines confidently. On the other hand, these experiences deepened my understanding of fundamental engineering principles, going beyond theoretical knowledge to include detailed, hands-on insights.

One project that left a lasting impression on me involved fully disassembling and reassembling a bicycle. I had no previous experience in mechanical work. However, through teamwork and step-by-step exploration, I eventually mastered this skill. Each project made us exhausted. There were many times when we returned to our dorms and fell asleep immediately after the sessions. Yet, there was an overwhelming sense of accomplishment. These hands-on experiences taught me that engineering is not just limited to theoretical deduction. What's more important is solving practical problems through real-world applications.

In my spare time, I actively enhanced my skills. Thanks to Beihang University's proximity to Zhongguancun, I frequently visited this area to purchase hardware equipment. I once bought a Raspberry Pi and conducted experiments by integrating it with various modules. I built small network tools with it and experimented with data transmission and network monitoring which helped me better understand the integration of hardware and software and proved invaluable when I wrote my graduate thesis on Mobile Ad-hoc Networks. Additionally, I independently developed a remote management tool based on the Linux operating system. This project deepened my understanding of operating systems and improved my network management capabilities.

Overall, these projects enabled me to apply knowledge learned in class to practice, laying a solid foundation for my subsequent academic research and future career development.

Cross-Cultural Exchange: From Student Union to the International Stage

Aside from my growth in technological skills and academics, cross-cultural exchange became an integral part of my experience. I had the precious chance of being a member of the student union, a role that offered me valuable opportunities to interact with students worldwide. Through these interactions, I deeply appreciated the unique charm of cross-cultural communication. Engaging with individuals from diverse backgrounds helped me develop a profound understanding of cultural differences and nurtured my respect for diversity. For example, while collaborating on projects with European classmates, I observed their meticulous approach to time management and their straightforward communication style during team discussions. And interacting with peers from different Asian countries revealed subtle cultural differences despite shared roots, such as varying attitudes towards collective glory.

Another memorable event was a cultural activity organized by the student union to introduce holidays of different countries. This activity allowed me to learn about the traditions of Malaysia, Indonesia, and other nations. In return, I introduced the customs and traditions of Spanish-speaking countries to my peers. These activities allowed me to immerse myself in diverse cultures and share mine. More importantly, they taught me how to work harmoniously in a multicultural environment, emphasizing that respect and understanding are the cornerstones of friendship and collaboration. Such cross-cultural activities were widely welcomed by students.

I also had several opportunities to present my professional knowledge on international platforms during my studies. As a researcher in information technology, I was invited to deliver talks at several international conferences. I vividly recall a conference in the Republic of Korea, where I was the keynote speaker. The presentation attracted attendees from various countries, sparking significant interest and discussions. Similarly, at a conference in Spain, I delivered a talk on the latest advancements in quantum cryptography, engaging in deep conversations with experts from around the globe. These academic exchanges introduced me to various research ideas and accomplishments in information technology, enriching my knowledge and firming my determination to further explore this field. I realized there is still a vast frontier of unknown to explore and many challenges to tackle within this critical field.

Alumni Bonds: Beihang University's Influence

One common experience is that whenever people realized that I could communicate in Chinese, they would curiously ask about my university. With the response of Beihang University, people would always comment with admiration, acknowledging Beihang University as an outstanding university. Whenever I encounter other Beihang University alumni, this shared connection instantly creates a sense of camaraderie and understanding. This invisible bond links us, and this alumni identity often opens doors to new opportunities, whether in professional development or collaborative projects. This recognition and the opportunities it brings make me feel fortunate and proud.

With the continuous pace of China's internationalization and Beihang University's dedication to fostering international collaborations, I am confident that more exceptional international students will join the Beihang University family in the future. They will gain profound academic knowledge, broaden their horizons, and experience the richness of Chinese culture, just like me. They will build lasting friendships with peers from diverse cultural backgrounds, promoting intercultural exchange and integration. On this platform, they will fully realize their potential, applying the knowledge and values acquired in China to contribute to the development of their home countries.

09

从河内到北京：追逐梦想的旅程

北京航空航天大学

阮氏清

　　阮氏清（Nguyen Thi Thanh），来自越南。2017 年，她开始在北航经济管理学院攻读国际贸易专业，在导师方虹教授的悉心指导下，她刻苦学习，不断探索，于 2020 年顺利完成学业。学习期间，她不仅专注于学术研究，还积极参与实习项目，在中国多家知名互联网公司实习，见证了中国互联网行业的快速发展。这些经历不仅拓宽了她的视野，也为她积累了丰富的实践经验。毕业后，她进入北京的一家跨国集团，在直播领域展现她的创造力与专业能力。对未来，她充满期待。

　　Nguyen Thi Thanh, from Vietnam, started her journey to obtain a master's degree in international trade at Beihang University in 2017. Under the guidance of Professor Hong Fang and through three years of hard work with continuous exploration, she got her master's degree in 2020. During her study, she not only devoted herself to academic research but also actively participated in many internships. She had the opportunity to intern and work in many well-known Internet companies in China, deeply contacting and understanding the rapid development of China's Internet industry. These valuable experiences not only expanded her professional horizon but also provided her with rich practical knowledge for her career. After graduation, she joined a multinational group in Beijing, focusing on live broadcasting, showing her creativity and professional skills in this emerging industry. She maintains unlimited expectations and pursuits for the future.

扫码观看
采访视频

中华文化的启蒙

我成长于越南河内的一个军人家庭。从小父母就对我要求非常严格，在他们的眼中，人生的道路清晰、稳定：考入一所优秀的大学，找到一份体面的工作，然后成家立业。然而，对于天生内向又喜欢幻想的我来说，这种固定模式让我感到有些压抑。小时候的我，不擅长与别人争论，也缺乏足够的自信去表达自己的观点。因此，我的童年虽然充实，但也略显单调。

因为毗邻中国，越南深受中华文化的影响。这些影响触及生活的方方面面。小时候，我们一家人经常坐在电视机前，观看中国的经典电视剧，比如《三国演义》和《西游记》。每次看这些剧集时，我都会对角色的命运和故事的起伏感到好奇。那些关于忠诚、智慧和勇气的故事深深吸引了我。我开始对中国的历史和文化感兴趣，不仅因为这些故事生动有趣，还因为它们让我看到了一种截然不同的价值观。

参观博物馆

在我小时候，河内的大街小巷常常有出租录像带的小店。每到周末，我和朋友们会省下零用钱，一起租几部喜欢的电影，围在家里的电视机前观看。这种简单的娱乐活动，是我们童年不可或缺的快乐时光。虽然那时的我听不懂太多汉语，但这些电影和电视剧里汉语特有的语调和旋律在我耳中成为一首首动人的歌曲。我和小伙伴们会尝试模仿影片中的对白，有时甚至会用一些简单的汉语词汇开玩笑。可以说，这段"影视启蒙"的时光在不经意间点燃了我对汉语和中华文化的热情。

社交媒体的兴起与新机遇的到来

大学时，我主修经济学。当时，学校的外语主要是英语，英语被认为是通向国际市场的"必备武器"。尽管英语的使用越来越广泛，我的兴趣却逐渐转向了汉语。我开始通过各种方式自学汉语，从简单的拼音到复杂的句子结构，每一点进步都让我充满成就感。

2011年，社交媒体已经开始改变像我这样的年轻人的生活。随着科技的迅猛发展，青少年能够从全球获取丰富的信息。当时，我的一位朋友是一名中国偶像的狂热粉丝。她不仅关注偶像的动态，还对中华文化产生了浓厚兴趣。我们经常一起看中国的综艺节目、电视剧，并尝试学习其中的一些日常用语。还有几位朋友已经获得了前往中国留学的机会，并从北京带回了许多有趣的故事。听他们描述在中国的学习和生活经历时，我既羡慕又好奇。这些故事让我开始思考：为什么我不能像他们一样，抓住机会去中国探索一个全新的世界？

于是，我开始和朋友们一起努力，并找到了一些关于国际奖学金项目的信息。我立刻被吸引住了，并为此积极准备。在大学课程之外，我们每天都会抽时间互相分享学习汉语的心得，激励对方保持动力。我们甚至为彼此制定了学习目标，比如每天学会5个新词，或者练习用汉语写一段小短文。尽管过程有些辛苦，但我们从未感到乏味，因为我们知道这份努力背后有一个激动人心的目标。

经过一段时间的准备，我鼓起勇气申请了中国政府奖学金项目。我选择了北航，这所大学以其卓越的学术水平而闻名。提交申请时，我的内心充满紧张，我每天都在幻想自己被录取的场景。收到录取通知书的那一刻，我欣喜若狂。那一刻简直不敢相信，我从未想过自己会如此幸运，能够在中国一所著名高校攻读国际贸易硕士学位。对我来说，梦想仿佛立刻就要成真。

说服家人：一项不小的挑战

虽然我对即将踏上这段旅程感到无比兴奋，然而，说服我的家人让我出国留学却并非易事。对于我要独自在一个陌生的国家生活，独自面对生活中的一切困难，我的家人感到很担心。

为了让他们放心，我特意准备了一份详细的计划书，列出了生活费用预算和学习期间的目标。我还分享了北航的背景资料，包括它的学术排名、国际学生支持体系以及我的导师信息。我告诉他们，这不仅是一次学术上深造的机会，更是一个让我成长为独立、坚强个体的宝贵机会。

经过耐心解释和多次沟通，我的家人终于同意并表示支持我的决定。他们的支持让我倍感温暖，也让我更加坚定自己的选择。我记得临行前，妈妈为我准备了一些家乡特产，还叮嘱我："无论走到哪里，都不要忘记家人永远在你身后支持你。"这句话深深印在我的心中，成为我在异乡奋斗时最大的动力。

北航生活：一段改变人生的经历

抵达北京的第一天，我就被这个城市深深震撼了。从机场到市区的路上，高楼大厦鳞次栉比，街道上车水马龙、井然有序。这一切都让我感觉到，北京不仅是一座有着悠久历史的古城，更是一个充满现代气息的国际化大都市。初到北京，我既忐忑又兴奋，迫不及待地想要探索这座城市。

在北航新主楼前合影

北航的校园更是让我惊叹不已。它既拥有现代化的教学设施，又有着浓厚的文化氛围。宽敞的校园绿树成荫，建筑风格融合了现代与传统，给人一种开放且包容的感觉。随处可见来自世界各地的学生，他们聚集在图书馆、自习室、咖啡厅里，讨论学术问题，分享生活点滴。这种多元化的环境让我意识到自己有太多需要学习的地方，也让我结识了许多志同道合的朋友。

更让我感到幸运的是，我遇到了学术导师方虹教授。她是一位严谨且充满热情的学者，在学术研究上追求卓越，同时也十分关心学生的成长。作为我的导师，她不仅在学术上给予了我极大的支持，还在生活上给予了我无微不至的关怀。刚开始时，我因为语言障碍和文化差异感到有些困惑和不安，方教授耐心地引导我，帮助我逐步克服这些困难。她鼓励我大胆提问、主动表达自己的想法，并要多参加校园内外的活动，以融入新的学习和生活环境。在她的鼓励下，我开始积极参加各种课外活动，包括学生论坛、学术讲座和文化交流等。在一次文化交流活动中，我代表越南学生展示了我们的传统

阮氏清（左）与导师合影

服饰和美食。这次经历让我深刻感受到文化交流的魅力，也让我更加自信地表达自己。在与不同国家的学生交流中，我学会了如何尊重和欣赏多样性。这种能力对我后来的学习和职业生涯产生了深远的影响。

在北航的第一年，我专注于完成专业课程，特别是国际贸易理论的学习。对我来说，研究生期间最难的课程是 C 语言程序设计，决定选修这门课程是因为我当时在一家互联网公司实习，对计算机是如何工作的十分好奇。在小组成员的共同努力下，我幸运地通过了考试，初步掌握了网络技术的基础逻辑。对于一个文科生，大家应该可以想象学习 C 语言有多可怕。北航的课程中，像 C 语言程序设计和电子商务这样的课程使我在工作中可以从另一角度获取新想法，为公司、为越南市场带来新的价值。基于对中华文化的热爱，我还选修了国际学院开设的汉语课程。那些时光对我来说是非常美好的记忆，尤其是冬天的清晨，我坚持早起去上课，不舍得错过。这些课程让我对中华文化有了更深层次的了解，使我受益匪浅。

硕士在读期间，我花了大量时间在图书馆阅读资料、完成论文，不仅掌握了专业知识，还培养了独立思考和解决问题的能力。随着时间的推移，我意识到仅仅学习理论是不够的，将知识应用于实践才能让我的学术更具价值。于是，为了获得更多实践经验，我开始寻找实习机会。通过学校的推荐和自己的努力，我非常幸运地获得了几家北京大型的互联网公司的实习机会。实习期间，我第一次近距离接触到了中国快速发展的数字经济。从参与数据

校园活动制作美食

分析到观察企业的运营模式，每一天我都会学到很多新的东西。印象最深的是在一次团队会议中，我大胆提出自己的看法，得到了团队的肯定。这次经历让我意识到，只要敢于尝试和表达，自己的能力就会被认可。这些实习经历让我不仅将课堂所学运用于实践，还对中国乃至全球的数字经济发展有了更深的理解。它们让我更加清楚自己的职业方向，为我后来进入职场打下了坚实的基础。

扎根北京

毕业后，我先后进入了几家知名的跨国企业，在不同行业和岗位上积累经验，我始终努力将自己在北航期间学到的知识和技能融入其中。

如今，我在一家大型互联网公司担任越南区域的运营经理。公司总部位于北京。作为连接公司与越南市场的桥梁，我的任务不仅是推动公司的国际化进程，还需要深刻了解越南本地市场需求，以制定最合适的运营策略。我的工作涉及多个方面，协调团队、优化业务模式、与客户沟通以及分析数据等。这份工作让我能够充分运用在北航就读时积累的宝贵经验，也让我有机会将这些知识带回我的家乡，为越南科技行业的发展贡献自己的力量。

在北京生活多年后，我感觉自己潜移默化地被中华文化改变了很多。刚到北京时，我对中国人的很多生活习惯感到新奇，比如早餐喝热粥、更爱喝温水等。随着时间的推移，我渐渐也习惯了，并发现这些方式对健康有很大的帮助。如今，我已经养成了每天早晨喝一杯温水的习惯，这是一种让我感到温暖的仪式，让我在开始一天的忙碌前感受到片刻的宁静。刚来时，北京冬天寒冷、干燥的气候让我感到不适。在朋友的推荐下，我尝试了中国人爱用的"泡脚"来缓解疲劳。这个简单的方法不仅让我放松身心，还让我感受到一种特别的归属感，仿佛融入了中国的日常文化。这些生活中的小细节让我更加理解中华文化的内涵，也让我在异国他乡感受到家的温馨。

在北京的生活

回首与展望

回顾我的旅程，我对塑造我人生的地方充满感激。从一个害羞的越南女孩到如今在职场上自信的女性，我走过了一段漫长的路。我希望我的故事能激励更多越南乃至世界各地的年轻人带着决心和勇气追逐自己的梦想。突破社会规范和家庭期望的束缚从来都不是一件容易的事情，但这往往是发现自身潜力的第一步和必要一步。

我衷心推荐大家来北航深造。北航学术成果卓越，同时为学生们提供了一个支持他们茁壮成长的环境。我非常感谢北航，特别是国际学院的老师们。他们不仅培养了我，还给了我一个与他人分享自己故事的机会。我真诚地希望未来能够以更有意义的方式为北航做点贡献，期待有一天我能够回到母校，重访这个让我梦想起飞的地方。

读者朋友们，我想送你们一句话：追随你的热情，相信你的能力，勇敢迈出追梦的第一步。这段旅程可能充满挑战，但收到回报后，你会发现所有努力绝对都值得！

导师寄语

　　纸上得来终觉浅，绝知此事要躬行。大学是学习的起点，而非终点。离开学校，踏进社会，是你人生新的起点。愿你在这个快速变化的时代，将终身学习、实践作为人生信条，不断吸收新知，持续自我成长，让智慧之光照亮你的每一步。

导师简介

　　方虹，北航经济管理学院教授、博士生导师，美国威斯康星大学密尔沃基分校高级访问学者。研究方向为国际经济与贸易理论、国际商务、经济全球化与当代中国经济、能源经济与管理。曾任中国高校经济与贸易类专业教学指导委员会委员、国际商务专业学位研究生教育指导委员会委员、中国国际贸易学会理事、中国服务贸易协会理事、中国市场学会理事，以及北航经济管理学院国际经济贸易系主任、低碳经济研究中心主任。主持国家自然科学基金项目 4 项、国家社科基金项目 2 项；主编《国际经济学》《国际贸易实务》《国际企业管理》《企业家精神与领导艺术》等教材。

The Enlightenment of Chinese Culture

I was born and raised in Hanoi, Vietnam, in a family with a long-standing military tradition. From a young age, I was brought up under the strict and disciplined upbringing of my family. In my parents' eyes, my life should be a very clear and steady trajectory, going to an outstanding university, finding a decent job and building my own family. However, for a girl like me, who is naturally introverted and likes to fantasize, this fixed pattern makes me feel a little depressed. When I was young, I was not good at arguing with others and lacked confidence to express my opinions. Thus, my childhood was fulfilling yet a little dull.

As a neighboring country of China, Vietnam has been deeply influenced by Chinese culture for generations. These influences extend beyond traditions and customs, touching many aspects of life. Traces of Chinese culture can always be found in Vietnam's culture. When I was a kid, my family often sat in front of the TV and watched classic Chinese TV series together, such as *Romance of the Three Kingdoms* or *Journey to the West*. I remember watching these episodes and always being curious about the fate of the characters and the ups and downs of the story. The stories of loyalty, wisdom and courage captivated me. I became interested in Chinese history and culture, not only because the stories were interesting, but also because they opened my eyes to a very different set of values.

When I was a kid, there were small shops providing video tapes for rent along the streets of Hanoi. Every weekend, my friends and I would save our pocket money to rent a couple of our favorite movies and watch them together. This simple pastime became an integral and happy part of our childhood. Through these movies and TV series, I had my very first understanding of the Chinese language. Although I didn't understand much Chinese at that time, the unique intonation and melody of Chinese sounded like a touching song in my ears. Gradually, I began to imitate the dialogues in the film, sometimes even using some simple Chinese words to joke with my friends. It can be said that this exposure to film and television inadvertently ignited my enthusiasm for the Chinese language and Chinese culture.

The Rise of Social Media and the Advent of New Opportunities

I majored in economics during my undergraduate study. At that time, English was mainly taught as a foreign language in university because it was considered necessary to enter the international market. However, although English was becoming increasingly widely used, my interest gradually turned to Chinese. I began to teach myself Chinese in various ways, from simple pinyin to complex sentence structures, and every step of progress filled me with a sense of accomplishment.

By 2011, social media had begun reshaping the lives of young people like me. With the rapid development of technology, teenagers were able to access a wealth of information from around the globe. At that time, one of my close friends was a devoted fan of a Chinese pop idol. She not only kept up with her idol's updates but also developed a strong interest in Chinese culture. We often watched Chinese variety shows and dramas together and tried to learn some daily expressions from them. Additionally, some of my other friends had already studied abroad in Beijing and returned with fascinating stories about their experiences in China. Listening to their descriptions of studying and living experiences in China, I felt envy and curiosity. Their stories planted an idea in my mind: why couldn't I pursue the opportunity to study in China and explore a new world, just like them?

From then on, my friend and I began working toward this dream together. We found some scholarship opportunities, which immediately attracted me and for which I actively began preparing. Outside of our university courses, we spent time helping each other improve our Chinese language skills and pushing one another to stay motivated. We even set learning goals for each other, such as learning five new words per day or practicing writing a short paragraph in Chinese. Despite the hard work, we never got tired because we knew there was an exciting goal behind the effort.

After a period of preparation, I plucked up my courage to apply for the CSC scholarship program. I chose Beihang University, which is known for its academic excellence. When I submitted my application, my heart was filled with nervousness. I spent weeks waiting for the results, fantasizing every day about what would happen if I was accepted. When I received the acceptance letter, I was overwhelmed with joy. It was a moment of disbelief. I never imagined I could be so fortunate. The opportunity to pursue a master's degree in International Trade at a prestigious university in China felt like a dream come true very soon.

Convince My Family: A Big Challenge

While I was thrilled to embark on this journey, convincing my family to let me study abroad was not a small feat. My family was worried about the challenges I might face living alone in a foreign country and managing everything independently.

To reassure them, I prepared a detailed plan outlining the contents of the scholarship, a budget for living expenses, and goals for my study. I also shared background information about Beihang University, including its academic rankings, international student support system, and information about my tutors. I told them that this was not only an opportunity to further study, but also a valuable experience for me to grow independent and strong.

Thankfully, after countless conversations and patient explanations, my family finally agreed to support me. Their support made me feel warm and determined. I remember before leaving, my mother prepared some local specialties for me and told me, "No matter where you go, don't forget that your family will always be behind you." This sentence is deeply imprinted in my heart and has become the biggest motivation for me to strive in a foreign land.

Life at Beihang University: A Transformative Experience

On my first day in Beijing, I was struck by the city. On the way from the airport to the city center, tall buildings are lined up and there is heavy traffic on the street running in order. All these made me feel that Beijing is not only an ancient city with a long history, but also an international metropolis full of modern atmosphere. When I first arrived in Beijing, I felt a mixture of perturbation and excitement, which made me eager to explore the city.

The campus of Beihang University is even more amazing, and it has both modern teaching facilities and a strong cultural atmosphere. The spacious, tree-lined campus and architecture blending modern and traditional styles provide an open and inclusive feel. Students from all over the world gathered in libraries, study rooms, and coffee shops to discuss academic issues or share life experiences. This diverse environment left me feeling both novel and excited, made me realize that I had a lot to learn and enabled me to meet many like-minded friends.

I was even more fortunate to have Professor Hong Fang as my supervisor. She is a rigorous and passionate scholar who strives for excellence in academic research and cares deeply about the growth of her students. As my supervisor, she gave me both great academic support and the best care in life. At the beginning, I felt a little confused and upset because of the language barrier and cultural differences, but Professor Fang patiently guided me and helped me gradually overcome these difficulties. She encouraged me to ask questions, express my ideas proactively, and participate in more activities inside and outside the campus to integrate into the new learning and living environment. With her encouragement, I actively participated in various extracurricular activities, including student forums, academic lectures and cultural exchange activities. In a cultural exchange activity, I represented Vietnamese students by showing our traditional clothes and food. This experience touched me deeply with the charm of cultural exchange and made me more confident about expressing myself. Through interacting with students from different countries, I learned how to respect and appreciate diversity, and this ability has had a profound impact on my later studies and career.

In my first year at Beihang University, I focused on completing courses, especially the study of international trade theory. For me, the most difficult course during my postgraduate study was the C Programming Language. I decided to take this course as an elective because I was interning at an Internet company at that time and was very curious about how computers work. With the joint efforts of my team members, I was lucky enough to pass the exam and grasp the basic logic of the network. As a liberal arts student, you can probably imagine how terrifying the C programming language was. In the curriculum of Beihang University, courses like the C Programming Language and E-commerce enabled me to obtain new ideas from another perspective at work and bring new value to the company and the Vietnamese market. Out of my love for Chinese culture, I also participated in Chinese courses offered by the International School, which left very wonderful memories on me. Especially in winter mornings, I persisted in getting up early to attend every class, never wanting to miss a single one. These courses enabled me to have a deeper understanding of Chinese culture and greatly benefited me.

During my master's study, I spent a lot of time in the library reading materials, finishing papers. I mastered professional knowledge and developed the ability to think and solve problems independently. However, as time went on, I realized that just learning the theory wasn't enough, and applying the knowledge to practice would make my academic background more valuable. To gain more practical experience, I began looking for internship opportunities. Through the recommendation of the school and my efforts, I was very lucky to get internship opportunities in several big Internet companies in Beijing. During the internship, I had my first close contact with China's rapidly developing digital economy. From participating in data analysis to observing how business operates, I learned something new every day. What impressed me most was a team meeting where I bravely put forward my own opinion and gained recognition from the team. This experience made me realize that if I dare to try and express myself, my abilities can be seen. The internship experiences not only allowed me to apply what I learned to practice, but also gave me a deeper understanding of the development of digital economy in China and the world. They laid a solid foundation for my professional journey later, pointing me to a clearer career direction.

Rooted in Beijing

After graduation, I successfully entered several prominent multinational corporations, where I gained valuable experience across various industries and positions. In these jobs, I have always tried to integrate the knowledge and skills I learned at Beihang University into practical work.

Currently, I am an operations manager at a large internet company based in Beijing and in charge of the operations in Vietnam. This role presents both challenges and opportunities for me. As the bridge between the company's headquarters and the Vietnamese market, my task is to push forward the company's internationalization process as well as to deeply understand Vietnamese local market needs to develop the most suitable operational strategies. My job involves various aspects, including coordinating teams, optimizing business models, communicating with customers, and analyzing data. This role allows me to fully utilize the valuable experiences I gained during my studies at Beihang University and provides me with the opportunity to bring the knowledge back to my hometown, through which I could contribute to the development of Vietnam's technology industry.

Having been living in Beijing for several years, I feel that I've been imperceptibly changed by Chinese culture. When I first arrived, I was fascinated by many Chinese daily habits, such as drinking hot porridge for breakfast and preferring warm water to cold drinks. Over time, I gradually adapted to these lifestyles and found that they were very beneficial to health. Nowadays, I have developed the habit of drinking a cup of warm water every morning, a ritual that provides me with a moment of calm before the start of a busy day. At first, the cold winter in Beijing made me feel uncomfortable, but after being recommended by a friend, I tried the Chinese traditional "foot bath" to relieve fatigue. This simple practice not only helped me relax both physically and mentally, but also gave me a special sense of belonging, as if I had integrated into China's daily culture. These small details in everyday life have helped me better understand the essence of Chinese culture and made me feel the warmth at home in a foreign land.

Look Back and Move Forward

Reflecting on my journey, I am filled with gratitude for the places that have shaped my life. From a shy girl in Vietnam to a confident professional, I've come a long way. I hope that my story will inspire young people—not just in Vietnam but also around the world—to pursue their dreams with determination and courage. Breaking through the restricts of family expectations and social norms is never easy, but it is often the first and necessary step to truly discover one's potential.

I strongly recommend students consider Beihang University for their studies. It is a place where academic excellence meets cultural enrichment, offering a supportive environment for students to thrive. I will always be grateful to the professors and staff, particularly the faculty of the International School, for not only teaching me but also giving me the opportunity to share my story with others. I sincerely hope that I can continue contributing to my alma mater in meaningful ways from now to the future. And I look forward to returning to this campus where my dreams took off one day.

To those reading my story, I have some words to share: Follow your passion, believe in your abilities, and don't be afraid to take the first step toward your dreams. The journey may be challenging, but the rewards will be worth all the effort.

Message from the Supervisor

Knowledge gained from books always seems shallow, only through personal practice can one have a profound understanding of it. The university is not the end of the study but the start. Leaving school and entering society is a new starting point in your life. May you take lifelong learning and practice as your motto in this rapidly changing era, constantly absorb new knowledge, keep improving yourself, and may the light of wisdom illuminate every step of your life.

Introduction to the Supervisor

Hong Fang is a professor and doctoral supervisor at the School of Economics and Management, Beihang University, and a senior visiting scholar at the University of Wisconsin-Milwaukee in the United States. Her research directions include theories and policies of international economics and trade, international business, economic globalization and contemporary Chinese economy, energy economics and management. She has formerly served as a member of the Teaching Steering Committee for Economics and Trade Majors in Chinese Universities, and a member of the Steering Committee for the Postgraduate Education of the Master of International Business Professional Degree. She is also a director of the China Association of International Trade, a director of the China Association of Trade in Services, and a director of the China Marketing Association. She once served as the Director of the Department of International Economics and Trade at the School of Economics and Management of Beihang University, the Director of the Research Center for Low-Carbon Economy. She has completed 4 projects supported by the National Natural Science Foundation of China and 2 projects supported by the National Social Science Fund of China. She has published several textbooks such as *International Economics*, *International Trade Practice*, *International Enterprise Management* and *Entrepreneurship and Leadership Art*.

10

飞雪连天求学路，笑书北航中非情

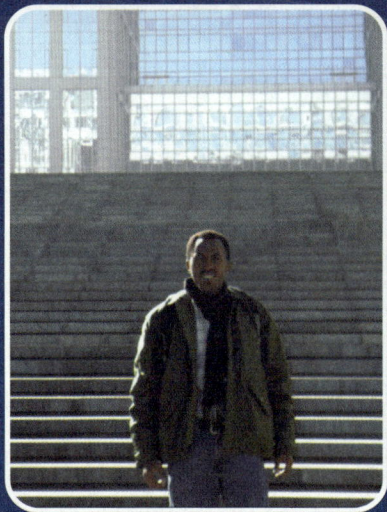

德 东

　　2010 年，德东（Kagabo Dieudonne）获得布隆迪政府的奖学金，来中国留学，进入北航攻读硕士学位，并最终在 2020 年获得博士学位。德东在北航度过了十年的学习时光，不仅获得学术上的成就，还深刻感受到中非之间日益紧密的教育交流与合作。博士毕业后，他选择回到布隆迪，从事教育工作，并在布隆迪大学和基加利大学担任讲师，同时致力于推动中布、中非之间的教育合作。

　　In 2010, Kagabo Dieudonne received a scholarship from the Burundian government to study in China. He pursued his master's degree at Beihang University and ultimately obtained his PhD in 2020. Over the course of his ten years at Beihang, Dieudonne achieved academic success while also experiencing the growing educational exchange and cooperation between China and Africa. After obtaining his doctorate, he chose to return to Burundi and engage in education work. He currently serves as a lecturer at the University of Burundi and the University of Kigali. He also dedicates himself to promoting educational cooperation between China and Burundi, as well as between China and Africa.

我叫 Kagabo Dieudonne，汉语名字是德东。我来自东非的布隆迪，也许很多人不太熟悉这个位于非洲大湖地区的小国，但它在我心中有着特别的意义。我的故事得从 2010 年说起，那时我有幸获得了一次改变人生的机会——来到中国，进入北航攻读硕士学位。在接下来的十年里，我不仅完成了硕士学习，还获得了北航的博士学位。

布隆迪少年的中国印象

回顾这段旅程，我想从最初的动机谈起。小时候，我从未想过自己有一天会来到中国留学。作为一个布隆迪的小男孩，我对中国最早的印象来自电影。在童年的记忆里，中国是一个充满神秘色彩的地方。我以为每个中国人都像电影里那样会功夫，身手不凡。那时的我对中国充满了憧憬和想象，功夫和武术深深植入了我的脑海。中国似乎和其他地方完全不同，它的文化、历史以及人们的生活方式都让我着迷。

随着我渐渐长大，我对中国的了解也逐渐加深。在高中和大学期间，我开始关注世界新闻，了解到中国的经济快速发展，基础设施建设稳步推进。特别是北京和上海这样的大都市，是全球经济框架中不可忽视的力量。那个时候，我的内心对中国充满了好奇和向往。我想亲眼看看这个高速发展的国家，亲身感受它的变化与活力。

机会终于来了。在我本科毕业后，布隆迪政府启动了一项出国留学的奖学金计划，专门为成绩优秀的学生提供深造机会。幸运的是，我成了其中的一员。当时，负责学生派遣的政府官员让我在摩洛哥和中国之间做出选择，我毫不犹豫地选择了中国。对我来说，这是一个实现童年梦想的机会，终于能够亲眼见证中国的繁荣与发展，看看中国是不是到处都是"武林高手"。

确定了目标国家之后，我着手准备申请学校的事宜。当时，我需要从中国的众多高校中选择 3 所进行申请。说实话，这并不容易，因为中国的高等教育系统对我来说是陌生的。我花了很多时间在网上研究，了解各个学校的课程设置、师资力量以及校园环境。经过一番仔细比较后，我被北航深深吸引。北航是一所以工科见长的大学，尤其在航空航天领域享有极高的声誉。而我对工程技术和科学研究充满热情，这与北航的优势不谋而合。尽管有朋友认为北京的生活成本较高，建议我选择其他城市的学校，但我坚持选择北航。我始终认为，北京作为中国的首都，拥有丰富的文化底蕴和优越的学习环境，是我实现个人梦想的理想之地。

终于，经过几周的等待，我收到了北航的录取通知书。那一刻，我的心情难以言表，这是我人生中一个重要的里程碑，我即将踏上新的征程。

初入校园的新奇与挑战

2010 年初到北京时，我的内心充满了好奇与期待。记得那天，我刚从飞机上下来，走出机场，迎接我的是一个截然不同的世界。北京的城市和建筑规模之宏伟远远超出了我的想象。到达北航时，我更加惊讶，校园里有巨大的教学楼，宽阔的马路，整个校园就像一座小型城市。我一度怀疑自己是否真的来到了学校，因为它的规模远比我在布隆迪见过的任何校园都要大得多。

学校的迎新工作做得非常好。当天，学校的工作人员和一些在校学生热情地接待了我们这些新生。我还记得那天郭老师亲自迎接我们，为我们安排宿舍，告知第二天迎新会的细节。校园内的设施非常齐全，有餐厅、超市、运动场，我感觉自己来到了一个全新的世界。

接下来的几天，我们参加了学校为国际学生准备的迎新活动。学校为我们提供了详细的校园地图，标注了各个教学楼、实验室和图书馆的位置。让我特别感动的是，学校还安排了一些学长作为我们的"梦拓"，帮助我们适应新的学习和生活环境。他们耐心地为我们解答各种问题，无论是选择课程，还是处理日常生活中的琐事，他们都给予我极大的帮助。这种关怀让我感受到北航的温暖与周到。

说实话，初到中国时，我有一些小小的失望。我发现，中国人并不像我小时候想象的那样，每个人都会功夫。许多中国学生和我一样，都是普通的年轻人，努力学习，追求自己的梦想。不过，尽管我的童年幻想破灭了，但中国人给我的真实印象却更深刻，他们勤奋、友好且非常有礼貌。在北航的学习过程中，我遇到了许多出色的中国学生和老师，他们的专业素养和敬业精神让我受益匪浅。我的硕士导师刘凯老师是一位年轻而才华横溢的学者。他在学术上非常严谨，对我的研究给予了细致入微的指导。每当我遇到

德东（右三）与学位论文答辩老师合影

难题时，他总是不厌其烦地帮助我寻找解决方案。我的博士导师姚忠老师也为我的研究提供了极大的支持。他不仅在学术上给予我指导，还在生活中关心我，帮助我克服了许多困难。

除了导师们的帮助，学校负责国际学生事务的老师们也让我倍感温暖。他们从我到校的第一天起就一直关心着我的学习和生活。不管是签证、学籍问题，还是生活中的琐事，他们总是第一时间为我提供帮助。这种无微不至的关怀让我在异国他乡找到了家的感觉。

我参加了多个学生社团，特别是文化交流社团。在社团里，我们一起策划文艺晚会，开展语言交流活动，让不同文化背景的同学们相互了解，增进友谊。这些经历不仅丰富了我的大学生活，也让我的组织和沟通能力得到了提升。每年举行的国际文化节给我留下了深刻的印象。在这一天，来自不同国家的学生穿着传统服饰，带着自己国家的特色美食，欢聚一堂。我们一起欣赏各国的舞蹈、音乐，还能品尝各种美食。这种跨文化的交流让我感到无比的快乐，也是我在北航生活中最难忘的时刻之一。

2012 年，我被国际学院选中参与组织北航 60 周年校庆。那天恰好是我的生日。在庆典上，我和同学们一起表演节目，还参与了许多丰富多彩的活动。能在这样一个重要的时刻与大家共同度过，那一刻，我不仅为北航感到自豪，也为自己感到骄傲。我们展示了不同国家的文化，欣赏了许多精彩的表演，观众们的欢笑和喜悦让我感受到了节日的气氛。

当然，在北航的学习也并非一帆风顺，我遇到过不少困难。攻读硕士学位期间，我在编程方面遇到了巨大的挑战，需要一点点地学习。起初，即使是理解基本算法或调试一个简单的程序，对我来说都很困难。然而，得益于北航全面的资源支持，包括学习平台、实验室和助教的耐心指导，我逐渐掌握了这项技能。我清楚地记得在实验室度过的一个个深夜，我与同学们合作完成复杂的作业，并寻求老师的建议。有时，我会感到挫败，但我知道，这些困难是成长过程中的一部分。通过不断努力，我的成绩逐渐提高，最终顺利完成了学业，获得了硕士学位。

　　除学业外，饮食的差异和语言的障碍也给我带来了一定的挑战。初到中国时，我并不习惯中餐的口味。最初的几天，我只能选择一些熟悉的食物来填饱肚子，慢慢地才开始尝试新的菜品。好在没过多久，我便喜欢上了中国菜，这种热爱一直持续到了现在。特别是火锅和

亲手包饺子

饺子，已经成为我心中不可替代的美食。语言也是一个大问题。硕士班的21 名学生中，只有我一个外籍学生。起初我们尝试用英语交流，但有时并不能完全互相理解。通过学校提供的汉语课程，我的汉语水平逐渐提高，最终能够与同学们进行流畅的对话。学校每周都有汉语课，课后我也有很多的机会与同学们练习口语。在实验室中，我努力用汉语与同学们讨论课题，虽然刚开始时常常犯错，但大家都很有耐心，乐于纠正我。

　　适应新环境的过程中，冬天的寒冷对我来说是巨大的困难。9 月和10 月感受到的温暖和舒适，在 11 月被寒冷所取代，那种感觉令我不知所措。幸好经过一段时间的适应和装备的添置，我逐渐习惯了北京的气候。记得有天早上，我迫不及待地打开窗户，看到整个校园被白雪覆盖的美丽景象。我立刻叫醒了我的室友，拉着他一起去外面玩雪。我们在操场上打雪仗、堆雪人，尽情享受着这个特别的时刻。我来自气候温暖的国家，这段经历让我深刻体会到冬季的魅力。

　　我结交了不少朋友，尤其是 5 位中国同学，我们会在节假日一起聚会，学习彼此的语言和文化。我们至今仍保持联系，通过社交媒体互道问候，分享各自的生活和工作经历。有一位同学现在正在美国工作，而其他人则在中国不同的领域发光发热，我们之间的友谊超越了国界。

从硕士到博士的蜕变

获得硕士学位后，我决定继续深造。当我被博士项目录取时，我面临了一次可以称为改变人生的学术挑战。作为一名具有信息技术（IT）背景的学生，我决定深入研究一个新的领域——电子商务，连接 IT 与商业的领域。这一领域的课程对我来说是全新的挑战，我必须在这些课程和核心研究之间找到平衡。为了跟上作业、项目和发表论文的节奏，我经常熬夜学习。通过坚持不懈的努力，我学会了将 IT 知识与商业原则相结合，并逐渐应用这种结合去解决实际问题，最终于 2020 年获得博士学位。

北航为我提供了一个既充满挑战又极具启发性的学术环境，让我有机会深入研究科技领域的复杂问题。课程内容的要求非常高，这促使我不断培养批判性思维，并将所学的理论知识应用于实际问题中。在这里，我不仅掌握了先进的技术和管理方法，还学会了如何通过跨学科的思维解决实际挑战。北航教授们丰富的学术经验和创新精神启发了我，他们的指导帮助我提升了独立研究的能力，开阔了我的学术视野。在导师的帮助下，我积累了宝贵的研究经验。这些经历不仅让我在技术层面得到提升，还锻炼了我的团队合作与项目管理能力，尤其是在与来自不同文化背景的同学们一起合作的过程中，我更加体会到了跨文化交流和协作的重要性。

学成归国，传递中非教育火种

中非之间的友谊深厚且广泛，不仅体现在经济合作和文化交流上，也体现在教育领域。中国长期以来致力于支持非洲国家的发展，尤其在教育领域不断投入和提供援助，帮助非洲许多国家培养了大量人才。作为一名曾在中国接受教育的学生，我深刻体会到中非友谊的深远意义。中国的教育理念和方法不仅开阔了我的视野，也激励我将这些宝贵的经验带回家乡，推动布隆迪的教育事业发展。在这个背景下，我更加坚定了回到布隆迪继续贡献自己力量的决心。2022 年，我回到布隆迪，并顺利申请到了布隆迪大学的教职。能够在这里任教，对我来说是件极为荣幸的事情。布隆迪与卢旺达毗邻，交通便利，我便也在卢旺达的基加利大学担任讲师。在这两个国家之间往返，不仅能够丰富自己的教学经验，还能进一步促进教育的交流与合作。我会继续将我在中国学习到的教育理念和方法应用到课堂中，为布隆迪的学生们创造更好的学习环境，帮助他们更好地应对快速变化的世界。

我深知，教育是国家发展的基石，而布隆迪的教育体系需要更多的创新与改革。通过我的教学工作，我希望能为学生们提供更多的机会，培养他们的创新精神和解决问题的能力，为布隆迪的发展贡献我的绵薄之力。

我还参与了一些关于电子商务的咨询项目。电子商务在非洲，尤其在布隆迪发展迅速。我希望能够通过这些项目，帮助当地企业更好地拓展市场，同时也为年轻人提供更多的就业机会。每当看到自己的学生努力取得成功时，我内心总是充满了成就感和自豪感。展望未来，我希望继续在教育

德东（左一）和学生参加商品交易会

领域深耕，并为布隆迪与中国之间的教育合作贡献自己的力量。我与布隆迪驻华大使保持着联系，并计划在布隆迪大学与北航之间建立更多的合作项目。

我始终相信，教育是改变命运的关键。中国，这个曾经在我的童年幻想中充满神秘色彩的国度，最终以它的真实面貌和无限机会在我的人生中留下了重要的印记。我见证了它的飞速发展，也亲身体验了它的文化和教育体系。回想起在北航的点滴，我感慨万千。对于现在正在北航学习的年轻学生们，我的建议是：保持谦逊，认真倾听老师的教导，努力学习，这将会在你们未来的职业生涯中产生深远的影响。无论你身处何地，扎实的功底和良好的态度将帮助你获得更多的机会。

回想在北航的这段时光，我心中充满了感激。这不仅仅是一段学术旅程，更是一次跨文化的深度体验。我从一个充满幻想的少年，成长为一个能够独立思考、具备全球视野的研究者。这一切，北航给予了我太多的支持和帮助。

我感激那些曾经帮助过我的人，正是因为有这些人，我才能在异国他乡找到归属，找到梦想的起点。

我深刻体会到，只有不断追求知识与进步，才能在快速变化的时代中立足。无论未来的道路多么坎坷，我都会怀揣对教育的热爱，继续前行。我期待将来能有更多的机会去探索不同的文化，继续我的学习与研究，同时也希望能够把我在北航的经验分享给更多的朋友，让他们了解这个充满活力的校园。

硕士生导师寄语

德东给我的印象很深，他勤奋、努力、认真。尽管没有多少专业基础，但他凭借自身的不懈努力，最终克服挑战，顺利完成了毕业论文。毕业后，他如愿以偿，从事了他梦寐以求、热爱的教育事业，希望他继续为他的学校与北航，乃至布隆迪与中国搭建交流合作的桥梁，奉献自己的光和热。

硕士生导师简介

刘凯，北航电子信息工程学院教授，博士生导师，IEEE 会员、中国电子学会高级会员。研究方向包括空间信息网络、下一代移动通信网、移动自组织网络、无线传感器网络、航空电信网、卫星通信网络等。2000 年 3 月起在静冈大学访学研究 1 年，2002 年 1 月起在伊利诺伊理工学院做访问学者 2 年，2015 年 2 月起在得克萨斯农工大学做访问学者 1 年，2018 年 10—12 月在密苏里大学圣路易斯分校做访问学者。近年来已发表论文 100 余篇，其中 SCI 收录 40 余篇、EI 收录 100 余篇，授权技术发明专利 60 余项、软件著作权 10 余项，获 2008 年教育部科学技术进步奖一等奖 1 项、2015 年度国家技术发明奖二等奖 1 项。主持、参与国家自然科学基金项目、863 计划、国家科技支撑计划、973 计划、

国家创新研究群体科学基金、国家重点研发计划、航天科技创新基金等项目多项。

博士生导师寄语

　　德东在我指导下完成了博士生涯的学习，经过 8 年努力他终于获得博士学位。在中国求学的日子里，他坚持不懈、勇于挑战、攻坚克难，不仅获得了学位，还开创了自己的事业。他在中国的故事不仅是个人奋斗的象征，也是中非友谊的生动写照。希望他继续以积极的心态迎接挑战，拥抱未来，用自己的才华和热情，为布隆迪和中国的友谊贡献力量，在多元文化的交融中继续绽放光彩。

博士生导师简介

　　姚忠，北航经济管理学院教授、博士生导师。研究聚焦于 AI 应用、供应链风险管理、电子商务系统等，同时涉及群体智能与人工免疫系统在经济管理中的应用。主持多项国家自然科学基金项目，如"零售商风险规避的二元渠道协调机制研究""社会化商务中的消费者行为和定价策略研究""信息产品和服务的定价策略与实证研究"等。在国内外知名期刊发表多篇论文，其中 SCI/SSCI 收录 60 多篇。编著《C 语言问答》《电子贸易技术：EDI》等图书，积极将学术研究成果应用于实际，服务产业发展。

My name is Kagabo Dieudonne, and my Chinese name is Dedong. I come from Burundi, a country in East Africa's Great Lakes region. It might not be familiar to many, but it holds a special place in my heart. My story began in 2010 when I was fortunate enough to receive a life-changing opportunity: come to China and pursue a master's degree at Beihang University. Over the next ten years, my academic journey continued from a master's degree to a PhD. In August 2020, I successfully completed my studies and received my doctoral degree from Beihang University.

A Burundian Teenager's Impression of China

Looking back on this journey, I want to start by talking about my initial motivation. In fact, when I was a child, I never thought I would study in China one day. As a young boy in Burundi, my earliest impressions of China came from movies. In my childhood memories, China was a mysterious place, and I believed every Chinese person was a skilled martial artist, as in the movies. At that time, I was filled with admiration and fantasies about China. Kung Fu and Martial Arts were deeply embedded in my mind. China seemed completely different from other places, captivating me with its rich culture, history, and way of life.

As I grew older, my understanding of China deepened. During high school and university, I started following world news and learned about China's rapid economic growth and booming infrastructure construction. Major cities like Beijing and Shanghai are indispensable forces in the global economic framework. At that time, my curiosity and longing for China grew stronger. I wanted to see this rapidly rising country for myself and experience its changes and energy.

The chance finally came. After graduating from university, the Burundian government launched a scholarship program that offered top-performing students the chance to further their studies abroad. Fortunately, I was one of them. The government official in charge of sending students abroad asked me to choose between Morocco and China, and I chose China without any hesitation. For me, it was a chance to fulfill my childhood dream and witness China's prosperity and development firsthand.

Once I had chosen my destination, I started preparing for my university application. At that time, I needed to select three Chinese universities among many to apply to. Honestly, it wasn't easy because China's higher education system was a new field for me. I spent a lot of time researching various universities online, reviewing their courses, faculty, and campus environments. After careful comparison, I was deeply attracted by Beihang University. Beihang University is a top engineering university, especially renowned in the field of aeronautics and astronautics. My passion for engineering and scientific research aligned perfectly with Beihang University's strengths. Despite some friends advising me to choose universities in other cities, citing the high cost of living in Beijing, I insisted on Beihang University. I believed that Beijing, the capital of China, with its rich cultural heritage and excellent academic environment, was the ideal place to achieve my personal dreams.

After waiting for several weeks, I finally received my acceptance letter. At that moment, I was overwhelmed with joy. It was a major milestone in my life, and I knew I was about to embark on a new journey.

The Novelty and Challenges upon Entering Campus

When I first arrived in Beijing in 2010, I was filled with curiosity and anticipation. I remember stepping off the plane, going out of the airport, and entering a completely different world. The scale of Beijing as a city and the grandeur of its architecture are far beyond my imagination. When I arrived at Beihang University, I was even more amazed. There are huge academic buildings and wide roads on Beihang University campus, and the entire campus is just like a small city. I even wondered if I had really come to a university because it was much larger than any campus I had ever seen in Burundi.

The reception work was very well organized. On the day of arrival, the staff and some senior students warmly welcomed us. I remember one of the teachers, Ms. Guo, greeted us in person, arranged our dormitories, and informed us about the orientation details the next day. The campus facilities were incredibly complete, with canteens, supermarkets and sports fields all available. I felt like I had entered a whole new world.

In the following days, we participated in orientation activities prepared for international students. The university provided us with detailed campus maps, marking the locations of academic buildings, laboratories and libraries. I was particularly touched when the school arranged for some senior students to be our mentors, helping us adapt to the new study and living environment. They patiently answered all our questions, and provided great assistance on both course selection and daily life matters, which made me feel the warmth and consideration of Beihang University.

To be honest, I was a bit disappointed when I first arrived in China. I found out that Chinese people weren't like the Kung Fu masters I had imagined in my childhood. Many Chinese students were just like me, young people working hard and pursuing their dreams. However, although my childhood fantasy was shattered, the real impression that Chinese people gave me was even deeper. They were hardworking, friendly, and very polite. During my studies at Beihang University, I met many excellent Chinese students and teachers whose professionalism and dedication greatly benefited me. My master's supervisor, Professor Kai Liu, was a young and talented scholar. He was very rigorous in his academic approach and gave me meticulous guidance on my research. Whenever I encountered difficulties, he would patiently help me find solutions. My PhD supervisor, Professor Zhong Yao, also provided great support for my research. He not only guided me academically but also cared about my life in China, helping me overcome many challenges.

Besides the help from my supervisors, faculties at the International School also made me feel very warm. From the first day I arrived at the university, they constantly cared about my studies and life. No matter whether it was visa processing, academic issues, or any daily life matters, they were always the first to offer help. This kind of attentive care made me feel at home in a foreign country.

I participated in several student clubs. In the clubs, we organized cultural performances and language exchange activities, allowing students from different cultural backgrounds to get to know each other and strengthen their friendships. These experiences not only enriched my university life but also enhanced my organizational and communication competence. The annual International Cultural Festival left a lasting impression on me. On this day, students from different countries dressed in traditional costumes, prepared their unique cuisine, and gathered to share their cultures. We enjoyed dances and music and tasted a variety of foods from around the world. This cross-cultural exchange brought me immense joy and was one of the most unforgettable moments at Beihang University.

In 2012, I was selected by the International School to participate in organizing the 60th-anniversary celebration of Beihang University, which just happened to fall on my birthday. During the event, I performed with my classmates and took part in many colorful activities. At that moment, I felt immense pride, not only for Beihang University but also for myself, as I was fortunate to spend such an important time here. We presented cultures from different countries and enjoyed many wonderful performances. The laughter and joy of the audience made me feel the festive atmosphere.

Needless to say, my time at Beihang University was not smooth sailing all the time. I faced many difficulties, especially in my studies. During my master's degree program, I faced significant challenges in coding and programming. Starting almost from scratch, I had to learn everything step by step. Initially, even understanding basic algorithms or debugging a simple program felt like climbing a steep mountain. However, thanks to Beihang University's comprehensive resources, including access to advanced laboratories, online learning platforms, and supportive teaching assistants, I gradually became proficient in this skill. I vividly recall spending long nights in the lab, collaborating with classmates on complex assignments, and seeking advice from professors. The courses in the engineering program were quite challenging, and the theoretical knowledge and practical skills required a significant amount of time to master. At times, I felt frustrated, but I knew these difficulties were part of my growth. Through continuous efforts, my academic performance gradually improved, and I successfully completed the courses, ultimately obtaining my master's degree.

In addition to academics, the challenges of food and language also posed some difficulties for me. When I first arrived in China, I wasn't used to the flavors of Chinese cuisine. In the first few days, I often chose familiar foods to eat, not daring to try new dishes. Fortunately, it didn't take long before I began to love Chinese food, and this love has continued until this day, especially hotpots and dumplings, which have become irreplaceable for me. Language was also a big obstacle. Out of the 21 students in my master's program, I was the only international student. At first, we tried to communicate in English, and sometimes we encountered difficulties in understanding each other. However, through the Chinese language courses provided by the university, my Chinese proficiency gradually improved, and I was eventually able to communicate fluently with my classmates. The university offered weekly Chinese classes, which gave me more opportunities to practice speaking with my peers. In the lab, I tried hard to discuss the research projects in Chinese with my classmates. Although I made frequent mistakes at first, everyone was very patient and willing to correct me.

Adapting to the new environment also meant facing the big challenge of the cold in winter. The warmth and comfort I felt in September and October were replaced by the chill of November, which left me at a loss. Fortunately, after a period of adaptation and the purchase of some additional clothes, I gradually got used to the climate in Beijing. I remember the first time I saw snow. On that morning, I couldn't wait to open the window and see the beautiful scene of the whole campus covered with snow. I immediately woke up my roommate and dragged him outside to play in the snow. We had snowball fights and built snowmen, enjoying that special moment to the fullest. I came from a country with a warmer climate, and this experience allowed me to feel the charm of winter.

I also made many friends, including five Chinese classmates. We met during holidays, learning each other's languages and cultures. I still keep in touch with them to this day. We occasionally connect via social media, sharing updates about our lives and work. One of my friends is now working in the United States, while others are shining and excelling in their respective fields in China. Our friendship transcends national borders.

From Master to Doctor

After obtaining my master's degree, I decided to continue my studies. When the PhD program accepted me, I faced what I would call a life-changing academic challenge. Coming from an IT background, I decided to delve into a new research area—e-commerce, which bridges IT and business. The lessons were entirely new to me. I had to balance them with my research, often burning the midnight oil to keep up with assignments, projects, and publications. Through perseverance, I learned to integrate IT knowledge with business principles, and I began to utilize this combination to address real-world problems. Finally, I got my PhD in 2020.

Beihang University provided me with a challenging and intellectually stimulating environment where I had the opportunity to delve into complex issues in the field of technology. The high academic standards of the courses pushed me to develop critical thinking skills and apply theoretical knowledge to practical problems. Here, I mastered advanced technical and management methods, and learned how to address real-world challenges through interdisciplinary thinking. I was deeply inspired by the professors' wealth of academic experience and innovative spirit. Their guidance helped me enhance my independent research skills and broadened my academic perspective. With the support of my supervisors, I continuously accumulated valuable research experience. This experience not only improved my technical skills but also sharpened my teamwork and project management abilities. Especially through collaborating with classmates from diverse cultural backgrounds, I have come to appreciate the importance of cross-cultural communication and collaboration even more.

Pass the Torch of Sino-Africa Education

The friendship between China and Africa is profound and extensive. It is manifested not only in economic cooperation and cultural exchanges but also in the field of education. China has long been committed to supporting the development of African countries, especially through investments and aid in education, which has helped many African nations cultivate many talents. As a scholar who has studied in China, I deeply understand the significance of the friendship between China and Africa. China's educational philosophy and methods have not only broadened my perspective but also inspired me to bring these valuable experiences back to my homeland and contribute to the development of education in Burundi. Thus, I am even more determined to return to Burundi and contribute my efforts to my motherland. In 2022, I returned to Burundi and successfully applied for a teaching position at the University of Burundi, which is a great honor. Due to the proximity and convenience of transportation between Burundi and Rwanda, I also serve as a lecturer at the University of Kigali in Rwanda. Traveling between these two countries allows me to enrich my teaching experience and further promote educational exchanges and cooperation. I will continue to apply the educational concepts and methods I learned in China to my lessons, striving to create a better learning environment for Burundian students and help them better adapt to the rapidly changing world.

I am deeply aware that education is the cornerstone of national development, and Burundi's education system still requires more innovation and reform. Through my teaching work, I hope to provide students with more opportunities, cultivate their innovative spirits and problem-solving abilities, and contribute my modest efforts to the development of Burundi.

I have also participated in some e-commerce consulting projects, a rapidly growing field in Africa, especially in Burundi. Through these projects, I hope to help local businesses expand their markets and provide more employment opportunities for young people. Every time I see my students make progress through their hard work, I am filled with a great sense of accomplishment and pride. Looking ahead, I hope to continue deepening my work in the field of education and contribute to the educational cooperation between Burundi and China. I have kept in touch with the ambassador of Burundi to China and planned to establish more cooperative projects between the University of Burundi and Beihang University.

I have always believed that education is the key to changing one's destiny. China, a country that was once filled with mystery in my childhood imagination, has left a significant mark on my life with its true appearance and endless opportunities. I have witnessed its rapid development and personally experienced its culture and education system. Reflecting on my time at Beihang University, I am overwhelmed with emotions. To the young students studying at Beihang University today, my advice is to stay humble, listen carefully to your teachers' guidance, and study diligently. This will have a profound impact on your future career. No matter where you are, solid knowledge and a proper attitude will help you seize more opportunities.

Looking back on my time at Beihang University, my heart is filled with gratitude. Life at Beihang University was not just an academic journey but also a deep cross-cultural experience. I have grown from a young dreamer to an independent thinker and a researcher with a global perspective. Beihang University provided me with immense support and guidance. I am grateful to those who helped me along the way. It is because of them that I was able to find a sense of belonging and the starting point of my dreams in a foreign land.

Throughout this journey, I have deeply realized that only by continuously pursuing knowledge and progress can we stand firm in a rapidly changing world. No matter how challenging the future path may be, I will continue to move forward with my passion for education. I look forward to more opportunities to explore different cultures, continue my study and research, and share my experiences at Beihang University with more friends so they can learn more about this campus, which is full of vitality and possibilities.

Message from the Master's Supervisor

I was deeply impressed by Kagabo Dieudonne's diligence, hard work and commitment to his studies. Although he had little professional research background before studying at Beihang University, he overcame the challenges and successfully completed his graduation thesis through his efforts. He has achieved his dream and is engaged in the educational career that he has always been passionate about after graduation. I hope he will continue to contribute his own efforts and enthusiasm to build bridges for the exchanges and cooperation between his university and Beihang University, as well as between Burundi and China.

Introduction to the Master's Supervisor

Kai Liu is a professor and doctoral supervisor at the School of Electronic Information Engineering, Beihang University, IEEE member and a senior member of the Chinese Institute of Electronics. His research interests include space information networks, next-generation mobile communication networks, mobile ad hoc networks, wireless sensor networks, aeronautical telecommunication networks, satellite communication networks. He conducted visiting research at the University of Shizuoka for one year starting from March 2000, worked as a visiting scholar at the Illinois Institute of Technology for two years from January 2002, at Texas A&M University for one year from February 2015, and at the University of Missouri–St. Louis from October to December 2018. In recent years, he has published more than 100 papers, among which more than 40 are indexed by SCI and more than 100 are indexed by EI. He has been granted more than 60 technical invention patents and more than 10 software copyrights. He won the first prize of the Science and Technology Progress Award of the Ministry of Education in 2008 and the second prize of the National Technological Invention Award in 2015. In addition, he has led and participated in a number of projects, including the National Natural Science Foundation of China, the 863 Program, the National Science and Technology Support Program, the 973 Program, the National Science Fund for Innovative Research Groups, the National Key Research and Development Program, and the Aerospace Science and Technology Innovation Fund.

Message from the Doctoral Supervisor

Kagabo Dieudonne completed his doctoral study under my guidance. It took him eight years of hard work to finally obtain his doctoral degree. During his study in China, he was persistent and courageous in taking on challenges and overcoming difficulties, which enabled him to grow step by step. He not only obtained the degree, but also started his own career. His story in China is a symbol of personal struggle as well as a vivid portrayal of the friendship between China and Africa. I hope he will continue to embrace the challenges and the future with a positive attitude, use his talent and enthusiasm to contribute to the friendship and cooperation between China and Burundi, and continue to shine brightly in the integration of diverse cultures.

Introduction to the Doctoral Supervisor

Zhong Yao is a professor and doctoral supervisor at the School of Economics and Management, Beihang University. His research focuses on AI applications, supply chain risk management, e-commerce systems, etc. He also delves into the applications of swarm intelligence and artificial immune systems in economic management. He has completed several projects supported by the National Natural Science Foundation of China, such as Research on the Coordination Mechanism of Dual Channels with Retailers' Risk Aversion, Research on Consumer Behavior and Pricing Strategies in Social Commerce, and Pricing Strategies and Empirical Research on Information Products and Services. He has published numerous papers in leading domestic and international journals, with more than 60 papers indexed by SCI/SSCI. He has compiled several textbooks, such as *C Language Q&A, E-trade Technology: EDI*. He actively applies academic research achievements to practice to serve the development of the industry.

11

青春飞扬在北航，国际文化续新章

李子祥

　　李子祥（Dodo Guy Kitto），来自印度尼西亚，他 2008 年来到北航，从汉语学习开始，一步一个脚印，学习刻苦，在北航先后获得本科和硕士学位。同时，他也用热情与才华感染带动周围的同学，实现了国际学生课外活动的多个"创举"。他在北航的故事不仅属于他个人，更是国际学生与北航国际教育共同的珍贵记忆。

　　Dodo Guy Kitto, from Indonesia, started his journey at Beihang University in 2008. Starting with Chinese studies, he worked tirelessly to earn his bachelor's and master's degrees at Beihang University. His enthusiasm and talents inspired his classmates, achieving several groundbreaking extracurricular initiatives for international students. These stories became cherished memories not only for him personally but also for the international students and Beihang University's international education.

扫码观看
采访视频

汉语学习之因

我是来自印度尼西亚（简称印尼）的李子祥，英文名是 Dodo Guy Kitto，中国朋友都亲切地叫我"嘟嘟"。我出生在印尼的一个普通家庭，我家是华裔家庭，在外我和朋友讲印尼语，偶尔也说英语，虽然在家里讲闽南话，但汉语对我来说依旧是一门非常陌生的语言。

随着中国与印尼之间的交往合作日益深入和紧密，印尼兴起了"汉语热"。记得在我读小学六年级时，学校开始讲授汉语课。在这股潮流的影响下，我在上高中时就做出决定，毕业后要到中国学习。我的父母看到了中国的快速发展，希望我能够学习汉语，通过学习汉语了解自己的文化根源，同时也希望我能有机会体验中国的教育和生活。

李子祥在北航学习

2008 年，我高中毕业，面临着申请中国高校的重要选择。我居住在印尼的苏门答腊岛，那里信息相对闭塞，网络也不是很发达。我是通过当地的一家教育机构了解到一些中国高校的信息。在众多高校中，我被北航的教学与科研实力，特别是在航空航天、管理科学与工程等优势学科的实力所深深吸引。如果说到中国留学是为我打开一扇窗，那北航可能就是窗外我可以自由翱翔的天空。在父母的支持下，我决定先到北航进修汉语，一边学汉语，一边考虑和规划自己的本科学习。就这样，我踏上了前往中国、求学北航的旅程。

我清楚地记得第一次来到北京的日子，那是 2008 年 9 月 15 日。那一天，我刚下飞机就感受到了强烈的文化冲击。眼睛里看到的都是汉字，耳朵里听到的都是汉语，这种感官上的冲击让我深刻意识到自己即将进入一个全新的文化环境。

在北航学习汉语是一个不断克服困难的过程。在老师的帮助下，我的汉语取得了飞速进步。在学习的过程中，气候给我带来了一些不适应和小惊喜。我的家乡是热带气候，常年高温炎热，而北京四季分明，特别是冬天，寒冷干燥。印尼学生通常会不适应穿着厚衣服与暖和的鞋子，所以看到上身穿着厚厚的羽绒服，光脚穿着拖鞋的"怪人"，一问准是印尼学生。寒冷的冬天里，生病对我们来说也是家常便饭。在北航，我经历了人生中第一场雪的惊喜，当我拉开宿舍窗帘，看到窗外是一片白雪皑皑、银装素裹的景象时，我的心情激动不已，恨不得马上拿起电话与远在家乡的父母和弟弟们分享。

本科学习新生活

通过在北航为期一年的汉语进修，我越发了解和热爱这所大学，于是，我向学校提交了本科入学申请，并顺利通过考试。2009年9月，我正式成为经济管理学院工业工程专业的一名本科生。

本科学习时最大的挑战是专业课上的一些术语，刚接触时看不懂也听不懂，更不要说透彻理解含义。对此，和其他国际学生一样，我就采用课前预习和课后复习的方法，通过查阅字典和借助翻译软件帮助理解。有时需要先做中英翻译，再把英语翻译为母语来理解。遇到不懂的问题，我多是向老师和同学请教。与此同时，我一直坚持汉语学习，因为我相信，汉语是我在中国生活和学习的基础。通过努力，我逐渐适应了大学的学习环境和节奏，学习成绩也稳步提高。

我喜欢音乐，尤其是唱歌。此外，我也很喜欢结交新朋友。来到北航之后，我发现学校有很多学生文艺社团，学校也支持鼓励国际学生参加各种文化交流活动。于是，我尝试加入中国学生的社团，也积极报名参加各种汉语活动和歌唱比赛。最初参加活动时，我的汉语水平还不是很高，但通过这些活动和比赛的锻炼，我的汉语水平得到了极大的提高。这些丰富多彩的课余生活，让我走出在国际学生公寓中独自学习的状态，融入同学之中，我的朋友圈越来越大。

参加校园歌手大赛

我在北航的"创举"

倡导成立国际学院学生会

我的个性比较开朗外向，喜欢和大家一起组织和参加各种活动。最初几次我和同学们都是自掏腰包，乐在其中。为了更好地为国际学生提供交流的平台，更加规范和有计划地开展各种课外活动，在国际学院谷老师的支持下，我们成立了国际学院学生会，我有幸担任了第一任主席。

这一职务给我带来了不小的挑战。学生会为来自不同国家的学生服务，文化差异成为工作中需要重点关注和解决的问题。在组织各种活动时，我们需要协调来自不同国家的同学的需求和意见，并通过活动促进国际学生之间的交流与融合。这不仅需要良好的沟通能力，还需要对不同文化有深入的了解。我逐渐学会了如何在多元文化环境中有效地开展工作，如何平衡各方需求，以及如何激发同学们的积极性。

学生会成立之初，我们遇到过语言沟通的问题。英语授课的同学大多不会讲汉语，汉语授课的部分同学英语不太好，为了让大家能互相理解，我们决定每次开会都使用中英两种语言。我负责汉语，副会长负责英语。我们当时还特意把英语和汉语授课的学生安排在同一个部门，让大家充分交流，共同合作完成任务。令我们欣喜的是，这种工作方式一举三得，既锻炼了我们的组织沟通能力，也提高了大家的汉语和英语水平，更重要的是增进了各国同学之间的理解和融合。

举办北航第一届国际文化节

创办国际文化节是我在学生会工作期间最引以为傲的一件事，每每回想起来，仍然记忆犹新，心潮澎湃。当时，我受同学之邀去参加其他学校的国际文化节，深受启发，认为北航也应该有这样一个展示各国文化的舞台。我们与杨老师讨论了我们的想法，国际学院非常支持我们的计划。于是，我们开始着手筹备第一届属于北航学生自己的国际文化节。

整个筹备任务紧张而艰巨。作为国际学院学生会主办的第一届大型活动，从经费预算到场地安排等，我们都没有太多的经验。在国际学院老师们的支持和帮助下，我们从不同渠道筹集资金、制订预算、控制成本；经过与学校保卫处、后勤等多个部门的协调，活动场地的申请得到了学校的协助和

北航国际文化节

批准。

　　我们精心设计制作了宣传海报、文化节专属 Logo 和一系列周边；我们向周围同学广发邀请，并通过同学之间的互相推荐，争取联系到每一位国际学生。此外，我们还需要确定文艺演出的内容、形式和时间安排，确保当天下午文艺演出的顺利进行。

　　当天，大家从凌晨就开始忙活起来。我们把租用的帐篷从国际学生公寓旁边的地下室搬运到绿园南边。为此我还借了送水师傅的三轮车来搬运帐篷，那忙碌的场景现在想起来依然历历在目。

　　一整天的活动吸引了众多同学和老师的参与，精彩和热烈程度出乎意料，国际文化节取得了圆满成功！国际学生展示各国文化，增进了中外学生之间的交流与理解，也为北航的校园文化增添了一抹亮丽的色彩。此后，国际文化节成为北航的一项传统活动，举办规模逐年扩大。我很自豪地得知，到 2024 年，国际文化节已经举办 9 届了。对我来说，第一届国际文化节永远是最珍贵的记忆。我为我们国际学生的这项"创举"感到骄傲。

在华深造，继续前行

　　本科四年级时，我获得了顺丰市场营销部门和企业发展规划部门的相

李子祥（左七）在本科毕业典礼上

关职位，我在两个部门都通过了面试并得到了录用意向，这次机会对我来说是很难得的。但在就业和继续深造之间，经过深思熟虑，我最终选择了继续深造。一方面，我对知识有强烈的求知欲，非常珍视在中国的学习机会，另一方面，这也是为了完成父母的心愿，做弟弟们的榜样，我要成为全家第一位研究生。我很自豪，我做到了！

我成功获得了中国政府奖学金，在北航继续攻读硕士学位，专业是管理科学与工程。研究生学习期间，我的导师单伟教授给予了我很大的支持与帮助。单老师不仅在课程学习、科研实践、论文写作等方面为我提供了很多指导，在生活和思想上也为我倾注了特别的关心和照顾。他时常会找我聊天，关心我的学习和成长近况，他还经常分享自己的经验和故事，给了我很多启发和鼓励，让我更加坚定地走自己的路。

突破自我之新尝试

2015 年，研究生毕业后，我加入中国铁路设计集团，回到印尼，参加了雅加达到万隆高铁项目的建设工作，这是中国—印度尼西亚合作项目，也是印尼首个高铁项目。我的工作主要涉及翻译、招聘、财务等。刚开始工作时，由于是第一次接触到物理和化学方面的专业词汇，为了做好工作，我每晚下班后都会自学相关内容，仿佛又回到了怀念已久的大学时光。正是有在北航的学习基础，我很快就适应了工作节奏与工作压力。同时，我也非常高兴能够利用自己在中国所学，参与中国和印尼两国的合作，贡献自己的力量。

工作之余，我一直考虑如何更好地发挥自己的能力，找到自己兴趣与工作的最佳结合点。我家开了一家小超市，从小父母就经常让我接触家里的生意，教我如何给客人找零钱、如何包装、如何点货、如何跟客户打交道等，所以创业成为我从小的梦想。虽然父母都希望孩子们能够在大公司上班，但是我一直相信，每个人的成功之路是不一样的，能够从事自己喜爱的行业，就是最值得也是最幸福的事情。

2018 年，我做了人生中的一个重要决定，我开始自主创业。立足所学的国际贸易专业，我公司的主要业务是为中国和印尼客户提供进出口服务。这是又一次突破自我的新尝试。自己创业与在公司工作是完全不同的体验，创业需要更强的责任感，需要及时处理客户的问题，24 小时与客户保持沟通。虽然我的公司规模还不算大，但我对未来充满信心。北航的创新基因深深影响了我，在北航的学习经历和社交基础也让我在创业中受益匪浅，我相信，通过不断地努力和尝试，我一定能够在印尼的商业领域中取得更大的成就。

我是骄傲的北航人

虽然毕业多年，我仍然时刻关注着中国与北航的发展，每每与北航的印尼校友、中国校友、老师联系和团聚，都是我最幸福的时刻，正是"北航"这个名字把我们紧紧联系在一起，我为自己身为北航校友感到十分自豪。

现在全世界的发展都离不开中国。小米、华为、五菱、海底捞等品牌已经在印尼随处可见。我相信以后还会有更多。到中国留学是我这辈子最正确的选择，同时也是我这辈子最珍贵的经验。我认为，教育和文化的交流是加深各国人民相互了解和信任的重要方式。在未来，我将尽自己所能，让更多的印尼学子了解中国，了解北航，我鼓励更多的印尼学生到中国学习，实现梦想！

导师寄语

　　我是李子祥本科与硕士阶段的导师。李子祥自本科起便展现出卓越的综合素质与非凡潜力。其性格开朗豁达，在交流中毫无阻碍，无论是学术探讨还是日常沟通，都轻松自如，这使他在团队协作中发挥着重要作用。本科期间，他在管理方面天赋异禀，积极参与各类活动，多次代表北航参加节目与比赛，凭借优异的表现屡获佳绩，为学校争得荣誉。尽管课外活动频繁，但他总能巧妙平衡学习与活动，合理规划时间，确保学业稳步推进。他荣获北航优秀毕业生，可谓实至名归。在他申请研究生时，我毫不犹豫地选择他作为我的学生，我深知他对知识有着强烈的渴望，他在研究生阶段展现出突出的学术素养与钻研精神，不仅取得优异成绩，还积极参与各类学术交流活动。希望他从北航出发，在国际舞台上绽放光彩，愿他在追求卓越的道路上不断前行，期待他的未来更加闪耀多彩。

导师简介

　　单伟，北航经济管理学院教授、博士生导师，副院长，创新管理与科技政策研究中心主任。中国技术经济学会理事、中国信息经济学会理事、中国企业管理研究会常务理事等。主要从事创新管理、数字经济、商务智能等领域的研究工作。曾在首尔国立大学和罗格斯大学从事研究工作。主持国家自然科学基金项目等 20 余项科研项目，获省部级科研成果奖励一、二等奖 6 项。在 *IEEE Transactions on Engineering Management*、*Journal of Business Research*、*European Journal of Marketing*、*International Journal of Hospitality Management*、*Technological Forecasting and Social Change* 和 *Information Technology & People* 等知名期刊发表高质量学术论文 100 余篇，其中 SCI/SSCI 收录 40 余篇，他引千余次。

Why I Began to Learn Chinese

My name is Dodo Guy Kitto, but my Chinese friends affectionately call me "Dudu". I come from an ordinary family in Indonesia. I used Indonesian and sometimes English with friends and spoke Hokkien (Min Nan dialect) at home for my family is an ethnic Chinese family. To me, however, Chinese was still a very unfamiliar foreign language.

As relations between China and Indonesia deepened, a "Chinese craze" emerged in Indonesia. I remember that when I was in sixth grade, our school introduced Chinese classes. Under this trend, I made a decision in high school that I would study in China after graduation. My parents, recognizing China's rapid development, hoped I could learn Chinese, connect with my cultural roots, and experience China's education and lifestyle.

In 2008, after graduating from high school, I faced the critical decision of choosing a Chinese university. Living on Sumatra Island, where information was scarce and the internet was limited, I learned about Chinese universities through a local educational agency. Among many universities, I was deeply attracted to Beihang University's academic and research strengths, particularly in fields like aerospace and management science. I felt that the opportunity to study in China was like a window opening for me, and Beihang University was the boundless sky where I could travel freely. With my parents' support, I decided to study Chinese at Beihang University first, using this time to plan my undergraduate studies. That's how my journey to study at Beihang University began.

I clearly remember the day when I first came to Beijing, which was September 15, 2008. The moment I got off the plane, I experienced a significant cultural shock. Chinese characters filled my sight, and Chinese voices surrounded me. This sensory overload made me realize that I was entering a completely new cultural environment.

Studying Chinese at Beihang University was a process of overcoming challenges. With my teachers' help, my Chinese improved rapidly. During my study, Beijing's climate brought both discomfort and delightful surprises to me. Coming from tropical Indonesia, where it's hot year-round, I wasn't accustomed to Beijing's distinct seasons, especially the cold and dry winters. Indonesian students usually don't adapt to wearing thick clothes and warm shoes. The strange person who worn a thick down jacket on the upper body and slippers on bare feet must be an Indonesian student. Getting sick in the cold winter often occurred to us. But, it was at Beihang University that I experienced my first snowfall. When I opened my dorm window and saw the world covered in a blanket of white, I was filled with excitement. I couldn't wait to call my parents and siblings back home to share this magical moment.

A New Chapter in Undergraduate Life

After a year of Chinese language studies at Beihang University, I grew more familiar with the university. I applied for undergraduate admission and successfully passed the required exams. In September 2009, I officially became a student at the School of Economics and Management, majoring in Industrial Engineering.

The biggest challenge I faced was that I couldn't understand some of the technical terms in my major at first. To tackle this, I adopted a study routine of previewing lessons beforehand and reviewing them afterward, as other international students did. I used dictionaries and translation software, often translating Chinese terms into English first and then into my native language to fully understand their meanings. Additionally, I frequently sought help from my teachers and classmates whenever I encountered difficulties. At the same time, I continued to focus on improving my Chinese because I firmly believed that proficiency in the language was the foundation for both my academic studies and life in China. Through persistent effort, I gradually adapted to the study pattern and pace in university and steadily improved my academic performance.

I have a passion for music, especially singing, and I also love meeting new people. After arriving at Beihang University, I discovered a variety of student arts clubs and learned that the university encouraged international students to participate in cultural exchange activities. I decided to join Chinese student organizations and signed up for Chinese language and singing competitions. When I first joined these activities, my Chinese was still not very fluent. However, through practice and participation, my language skills have improved significantly. These vibrant extracurricular experiences helped me transition from studying alone in the international student dormitory to fully integrating into the campus community, expanding my social circle.

My Pioneering Achievements at Beihang University

Advocate the Establishment of the International School Student Union

Being an outgoing and enthusiastic person, I enjoyed organizing and participating in various activities. Initially, we often had to cover expenses ourselves, and everyone took part with great enthusiasm. To better serve international students and provide a more structured platform for extracurricular activities, we established the International School Student Union with the support of Teacher Gu. I was honored to serve as the first president.

This role brought significant challenges. The student union aimed to serve students from different countries, and cultural differences became a key issue we needed to address. While organizing activities, we had to balance the needs and opinions of students from various backgrounds. Our goal was to use these events to foster communication and integration among international students, which required not only strong communication skills but also a deep understanding of different cultures. Over time, I learned how to work effectively in a multicultural environment, balance different perspectives, and inspire participation.

In the early days of the student union, the language barrier was a significant issue. Students in English-taught programs often didn't speak Chinese, while some in Chinese-taught programs struggled with English. To ensure effective communication, we decided to conduct meetings in both Chinese and English. I chaired the Chinese meetings, while the vice president handled the English ones. We also deliberately assigned students from different language groups to the same departments to encourage collaboration. This approach proved highly effective. Not only did it enhance our organizational and communication skills, but it also improved everyone's Chinese and English proficiency while fostering mutual understanding and cooperation among students from different countries.

Hold Beihang University's First International Cultural Festival

One of my proudest achievements during my time in the student union was initiating the International Cultural Festival. I was inspired after attending a similar festival at another university and felt that Beihang University deserved its own platform to showcase diverse cultures. With support from Teacher Yang and the International School, we began preparations for the first International Cultural Festival.

The planning process was both intense and challenging. As the student union's first large-scale event, we had little experience with tasks like budgeting and venue arrangements. With assistance from the International School faculty, we sought funding from various sources, created a detailed budget, and coordinated with campus departments like security and logistics to secure approvals and support for the event.

For the festival's organization, we elaborately designed posters, a festival-exclusive logo, and merchandise items. We invited students from different countries to participate, reaching out through personal connections and recommendations. We also planned and scheduled performances to ensure a smooth program of cultural presentations during the festival.

On the day, we began preparations early in the morning. We rented tents and transported them from the basement near the international student dormitory to the Green Garden. I even borrowed a delivery tricycle from a water delivery staff to help move the tents. The scene remains vivid in my memory.

The festival exceeded all expectations, attracting a large number of students and faculty. It was a resounding success, not only showcasing the cultures of various countries but also promoting exchange and understanding between Chinese and international students. It added a vibrant touch to Beihang University's campus culture. The International Cultural Festival has since become a cherished annual tradition, growing larger each year. I'm thrilled to know that the 2024 festival marked its 9th edition. For me, the first International Cultural Festival will always hold a special place in my heart, and I'm proud of the contributions we made as international students.

Furthering My Studies in China

In the fourth year of my undergraduate studies, I had the opportunity to work at SF Express. After successfully passing interviews for both the Marketing and Corporate Development departments, I received two offers. This opportunity was incredibly valuable to me. When it came time to choose between pursuing a career or furthering my education, I ultimately decided to continue my studies. This decision stemmed from my thirst for knowledge and my deep appreciation for the opportunities provided by studying in China. Additionally, as the eldest son in my family, I felt a responsibility to set an example for my younger brothers and fulfill my parents' hopes of becoming the first to obtain a postgraduate degree in my family. I'm proud to say that I achieved this goal.

I applied for and was awarded the CSC scholarship to pursue a master's degree in Management Science and Engineering at Beihang University. During my postgraduate studies, I received immense support and guidance from my supervisor, Professor Wei Shan. He not only provided me with valuable direction in coursework, research, and thesis writing, but also took a personal interest in my growth and well-being. He often shared his experiences and wisdom with me, offering encouragement and inspiration that strengthened my resolve to follow my path.

New Attempt to Break Through Himself

After completing my master's degree in 2015, I joined the China Railway Design Corporation and returned to Indonesia to work on the Jakarta-Bandung High-Speed Railway project. This was a historic collaboration between China and Indonesia and the first high-speed railway in Indonesia. My work primarily involved translation, recruitment, and finance. Initially, I encountered many technical terms in physics and chemistry that were unfamiliar to me. To adapt, I studied these topics after work, reminiscent of my university days. Thanks to my solid educational foundation and experiences at Beihang University, I quickly met the project's needs and adapted to the high-pressure environment. I felt immense pride in applying what I had learned in China to this significant collaboration between the two countries.

In my spare time, I began reflecting on how I could better align my skills and passions. My family owned a small grocery store, so my parents often encouraged me to help out from an early age. I learned how to give customers the correct change, package goods, restock inventory, and interact with clients. Thus, entrepreneurship has been a dream of me since childhood. Although my parents initially hoped I would work for a large company, I firmly believed that everyone has their own path to success. To me, pursuing a career in an industry I love is the most fulfilling and meaningful choice.

In 2018, I made a life-changing decision. I started my own business. Drawing on my knowledge of international trade, I established a company that provides import and export services for Chinese and Indonesian clients. This marked a step toward self-discovery and personal growth. Running a business is entirely different from working for a company. Entrepreneurship requires a heightened sense of responsibility. I might receive a client call at any hour and need to resolve issues promptly. Although my company is not yet large, I remain confident about the future. Beihang University's culture of innovation has profoundly influenced me. My experiences and connections from Beihang University have also been invaluable in my entrepreneurial journey. By continuously striving and experimenting, I'm confident that I can achieve greater success in Indonesia's business landscape.

A Proud Member of the Beihang University Family

Although it has been years since I graduated, I continue to closely follow the development of China and Beihang University. Every time I reunite with Beihang University's Indonesian alumni, Chinese classmates, or professors, I feel a deep sense of happiness and connection. The name *Beihang University* has tied us all together, and I am incredibly proud to be a part of this family.

Today, the world's progress is inseparable from China. Brands like Xiaomi, Huawei, Wuling, and Haidilao can now be seen everywhere in Indonesia, and I believe even more will follow. Studying in China was the best decision I have ever made and remains the most valuable experience of my life. I firmly believe that education and cultural exchanges are vital ways that deepen understanding and trust between nations. In the future, I will do everything I can to help more Indonesian students discover China and Beihang University, encouraging them to pursue their dreams there and achieve their full potential.

Message from the Supervisor

I am the supervisor of Dodo Guy Kitto for both his undergraduate and postgraduate studies. Since his undergraduate years, Dodo Guy Kitto has demonstrated outstanding comprehensive qualities and extraordinary potential. He has a cheerful and open-minded personality, with no obstacles in communication. Whether it's academic discussions or daily exchanges, he can handle them with ease, which enables him to play an important role in team cooperation. During his undergraduate period, he had a remarkable talent in management. He actively participated in various activities, represented Beihang University in many programs and competitions, and won numerous honors with his excellent performances, thus winning glory for the school. Despite his frequent participation in extracurricular activities, he always managed to skillfully balance his studies and activities, plan his time reasonably, and ensure the steady progress of his academic studies. He deservedly won the title of Outstanding Graduate of Beihang University. When he applied for postgraduate studies, I didn't hesitate to choose him as my student. I was well aware that he had a strong thirst for knowledge. During his postgraduate stage, he demonstrated outstanding academic accomplishments and a spirit of dedication to research. He not only achieved excellent academic results, but also actively participated in various activities. I hope that starting from Beihang University, he will shine brightly on the international stage and continue to move forward on the path of striving for excellence. I anticipate an even more colorful and promising future for him.

Introduction to the Supervisor

Wei Shan is a professor, doctoral supervisor and deputy dean at the School of Economics and Management, Beihang University, where he also serves as director of the Research Center for Innovation Management and Science & Technology

Policy. He holds multiple professional affiliations including council member of the Chinese Society of Technology Economics, council member of the China Information Economics Society, and executive council member of the Chinese Institute of Business Administration. His research expertise spans innovation management, digital economy, and business intelligence. He has conducted academic residencies at Seoul National University and Rutgers University. As a principal investigator, he has completed more than 20 research projects, including 4 projects supported by the National Natural Science Foundation of China. His scholarly contributions have been recognized with 6 provincial/ministerial-level research achievement awards. He has published more than 100 high-quality papers in leading peer-reviewed journals such as *IEEE Transactions on Engineering Management*, *Journal of Business Research*, *European Journal of Marketing*, *International Journal of Hospitality Management*, *Technological Forecasting and Social Change*, and *Information Technology & People*. Notably, over 40 of these publications are indexed by SCI/SSCI, collectively receiving more than 1,000 citations.

12

"巴铁"情深，北航筑梦

北京航空航天大学

比 汉

　　来自巴基斯坦的比汉（Bilal Anwar）于 2011 年进入北航，攻读机械制造及其自动化专业。学习期间，他不仅在学术上追求卓越，还通过实践项目积累了丰富的专业经验，为未来的职业道路奠定了坚实基础。2019 年，比汉完成了本科和硕士阶段的学业，开启了人生新篇章。如今，他在一家公司的汽车部门工作，将他在北航所学的专业知识和跨文化沟通技巧应用在工作中。

　　Bilal Anwar, hailing from Pakistan, joined Beihang University in 2011 and majored in Mechanical Manufacturing and Automation. During his stay, he excelled academically and gained valuable hands-on experience through practical projects, laying a solid foundation for his future professional endeavors. In 2019, Bilal completed his bachelor's and master's degrees and embarked on a new chapter of his life. Now, he works in the automotive division of a company, where he continues to apply the professional knowledge and cross-cultural communication skills he acquired at Beihang University.

我叫比汉，来自巴基斯坦。2010 年，怀揣着对未来的美好期许和对知识的渴望，我告别了家乡，踏上了前往中国的旅程。我的目的地是在学术界享有盛名的北航，在那里我完成了机械制造及其自动化专业的学习。在这段历程中，我不仅实现了学术上的成长，也在这片土地上找到了终身的归宿。

抵达中国：感受文化差异

之前，我对中国的了解仅限于教科书中的一些历史和经济数据。我知道中国正在崛起为全球经济和技术大国，但对我来说，这片陌生的土地依然笼罩在神秘的面纱下。2010 年，我第一次踏上中国的土地。北京令我感到震撼，高耸的摩天大楼、井然有序的交通、浓厚的科技氛围让我既兴奋又紧张。

在最初的几个月，我不得不适应巨大的文化差异。从巴基斯坦的乡村生活到中国现代都市生活，我仿佛进入了一个完全不同的世界。尽管我有一定的英语基础，但耳边充斥着汉语，让我在某些时候感到无措。我下定决心要学习汉语，因为我知道语言是进入新文化的钥匙。

我开始了一年的汉语学习。课程结构合理，基础的拼音、语法、日常对话都涵盖其中。渐渐地，我克服了最初的紧张和不安，能够与同学和老师进行基本的交流。在学会几个简单的问候语后，每次用汉语跟人打招呼，都有一种特别的成就感，因为我知道自己正在克服障碍，慢慢融入这个充满机会的国家。

除了语言，文化差异也是一个挑战。在巴基斯坦，我们的日常生活充满着家庭聚餐和亲戚走访这样的社交活动。中国人也注重家庭与亲情，但整体上更注重效率和时间。北京快节奏的生活增加了我的压力，地铁高峰时段人潮拥挤，课堂时间严格管理。我意识到，我必须调整自己的生活方式，适应中国的节奏。

追逐梦想：在北航的学习

我的梦想是成为一名机械工程师。经过一番调研，我了解到北航在机械制造领域有着强大的师资力量和学术资源。2011年，我正式入学北航，成为机械制造及其自动化专业的本科生。美丽的校园，现代化的教学设施让我感到惊喜。在这里，我接触到了前沿技术，参与了许多具有挑战性的研究项目。

北航的课程设置紧凑且富有挑战性，尤其是在机械制造领域，理论知识与实际应用紧密结合。每门课程不仅仅局限于课本上的理论，还包括实验室的实践操作。我记得在一门关于机器人控制与自动化的课程中，我和我的团队设计并制造了一个机械臂。这个机械臂能够在复杂环境中自动执行任务。从设计到实现，每一步都是一个挑战，也让我真正理解了机械制造的精妙之处。

我选修了多门对我的职业发展产生深远影响的课程。其中最重要的一门课是材料力学，这门课程详细探讨了材料的各种特性。这不仅加深了我对理论知识的理解，也启发了我后来的研究方向——汽车车身冷冲压模具设计。对我来说最难的一门课是电路分析。我积极向教授寻求帮助，与同学们组成学习小组，还充分利用学校丰富的资源帮助我更好地理解课程内容。在教授和同学的帮助下，我最终在这门课程中取得了优异成绩。

比汉（左三）在奖学金颁奖典礼上

本科生阶段，我的导师王秀凤教授不仅给我提供了学术上的指导，还非常关心我的个人发展。我的毕业论文题目是"利用板材成形方法设计先进的汽车车身"。在她的支持下，我有机会与比亚迪研发部门的工程师合作，使用 SolidWorks 和 UG 软件完成设计。通过与比亚迪的合作，我们设计了先进的汽车车身，并在比亚迪制造工厂进行了多次实物实验。

在我的研究生阶段，彭翀教授引导我进入了更深层次的研究领域。他鼓励我在学术上进行创新，并教会我如何将理论知识与实践相结合。我的研究课题是"利用激光冲击处理技术提高航空发动机齿轮的使用寿命"。在研究过程中，彭教授为我提供机会访问清华大学等著名高校的实验室，与其专家、工程师合作，这让我接触到了国际领先的研究方法和技术。这些宝贵的

比汉（右）和导师在硕士学位论文答辩现场

经历促进了我在学术上的进步，提升了我的实践能力。我还参与了许多前沿的研究项目，其中一个重要项目是设计和开发自主飞行的无人机控制系统，该项目要求我们设计一种能够在复杂环境中自主飞行的无人机。我与团队成员一起通过无数实验和改进，最终取得了满意的成果。

在北航学习期间，我有幸加入了国际学院学生会，并在学生会的多个部门工作。2014—2015 学年，我荣幸地担任本科生学生会副主席。硕士研究生期间，我还担任了研究生会主席。在国际学院的支持下，我们举行了丰富多彩的课余活动。例如，我们组织了各类体育比赛和文化节活动，安排前往不同的城市进行户外拓展，参观中国先进的实验室以及历史文化遗址。这些活动不仅丰富了学生的课余生活，也增强了他们对中华文化和科技成就的了解。担任学生会主席的经历让我获得了宝贵的技能，如团队协调、活动策划和跨文化交流等。这些技能在我之后的职业生涯中发挥了重要作用。

和国际学院研究生学生会的同学在一起

文化融入：在中国的生活

作为一名国际学生，我在中国的生活不仅仅是为了学业，更是与这个国家深度沟通和融合。北京这座城市拥有深厚的历史底蕴，同时又是一个现代化的大都市。在我的空闲时间，我喜欢和朋友一起探索这座城市。我们参观历史文化遗址，如故宫和天坛，同时也体验现代的购物中心，参观高科技展览。中国的科技发展极为迅速，每次参观高科技展览时，我都能感受到中国在技术创新方面的巨大力量。

我还深深地喜爱上了中国的美食。尤其是在寒冷的冬天，我喜欢和朋友们一起出去吃火锅，辛辣的味道总能让我忘却一周的疲惫。

小小使者：中巴友谊的桥梁

在中国学习的几年里，我见证了中国经济的快速发展。特别是在"一带一路"倡议推出后，我看到了中巴经济走廊（CPEC）给巴基斯坦带来的巨大变化。CPEC 极大地促进了中巴两国在经济、贸易和技术等多个领域的合作。从能源基础设施建设到交通网络的升级，CPEC 为巴基斯坦带来了前所未有的发展机会。作为一名巴基斯坦人，我感到无比自豪和激动，我看到了我的祖国从这个伟大的合作项目中受益。

我经常关注 CPEC 的进展。每当看到新项目启动或重大工程完成的新闻时，我都会和中国朋友讨论，思考这些项目对两国的重要意义。特别是对于巴基斯坦，能源和交通领域的大规模项目有效缓解了当地的能源危机和交通瓶颈，改善了居民的生活质量。CPEC 之前，巴基斯坦每天停电 12 小时，但现在我们的电力充足，全天 24 小时供应工业运作。巴基斯坦北部的货物现在可以在一天内到达卡拉奇港，也是得益于 CPEC 建设的先进高速公路。我意识到，作为一名国际学生，我不仅可以学习中国的先进技术，还可以为两国之间的合作与发展作出贡献。我决定留在中国，我认识到，作为一名巴基斯坦人，我有双重责任：一方面，我必须回报祖国，为巴基斯坦的发展贡献力量；另一方面，我希望促进中巴两国人民更多的沟通与合作。

职业起点：我的北航烙印

作为一名在中国学习和生活多年的巴基斯坦学生，中国的快速发展给我留下了深刻的印象。我清晰地记得第一次看到中国高铁的情景，我在北京北站，看到大批乘客在高铁站匆忙穿梭。高铁的现代化、流线型设计仿佛在向我讲述中国在交通领域飞速崛起的故事。如今，中国的高铁网已成为世界上最大的一张铁路网，连接着各种规模的城市，使得出行高效便捷。这一基础设施不仅体现了中国的技术实力，也展示了中国政府在推动经济发展的决心和效率。

除了交通，中国在其他领域的技术创新与进步同样令人钦佩。在北航求学期间，我亲眼见证了中国在 AI、5G 技术和电子商务等领域的快速发展。无论是在课堂上，还是在与同学们的讨论中，我都能感受到中国学生对技术的热情以及对未来的无限想象。在我看来，中国的快速发展不仅仅是数字的增长和指标的提升，更代表着一个国家在全力向世界展示自己。

我深深感谢北航提供的高质量教育和丰富的学术资源。北航严谨的学术氛围培养了我对技术的敏锐洞察力和创新思维，让我在踏入职场时拥有了显著的优势。毕业后，我有幸加入了上汽集团，一家在汽车出口方面处于领先地位的公司。上汽集团专注于智能制造和自动化，这与我在北航所学的专业高度契合。作为一名工程师，我参与了多个大型项目的研究、开发和实施工作，例如在巴基斯坦拉合尔建立 MG 汽车制造厂。这些项目不仅服务于中国市场，还延伸到其他"一带一路"共建国家。

如今，我在一家中外合资公司工作，我们在中国和海外都进行汽车制造。在工作中，我应用了在北航学到的理论知识，同时也从中国同事更为精细和现代化的工作方法中学习。中国的制造技术处于世界领先水平，特别是在自动化、AI 和工业机器人等领域。参与这些项目让我感到无比自豪，因为我不仅是这些技术的受益者，也在推动中巴之间的技术合作。

在未来的工作中，我希望继续发挥我的专业优势，为"一带一路"共建和 CPEC 建设贡献更多力量。同时，我也希望通过个人的努力，促进中巴两国更多的科技交流。我相信，科技创新是两国合作的关键，教育和人才培养构成了这一合作的基础。北航为我打下了坚实的基础，使我能够在职业生涯中不断进步。我希望未来有更多的巴基斯坦学生来到中国，尤其是来到像北航这样的顶尖大学，学习世界一流的技术和知识。

结语：在北航的难忘岁月

回顾这段旅程，从最初来到中国时的茫然与不安，到如今有了自己的事业和家庭，我深知这一切都离不开北航的培养和中国为我提供的机会。北航不仅是我的母校，更是我人生中最重要的转折点。

直到今天，我仍然常常回忆起在北航的时光——课堂上与教授讨论，实验室里与同学们合作，以及校园中那段充满活力的日子。这些宝贵的记忆塑造了今天的我，也指引着我未来的道路。我知道，无论我走得多远，北航和中国将永远是我心中重要的家。

外国留学生奖学金颁奖现场

导师寄语

比汉是一位帅气大方的巴基斯坦小伙子，也是我指导的第一位硕士国际学生。初次见面，我就惊讶于他汉语的流利，对于学习的热情和对于中国的喜爱。之后的相处中，更是越发感受到他身上具备的诸多闪光点。比汉友善勤奋、谦虚乐观，他在取得优良学业成绩的同时，还担任国际学生研究生会主席。我们也常常得以在忙碌紧张的科研闲暇，听他谈起如何协调、沟通不同文化背景的同学间的有趣故事。

毕业后，我们一直保持着联系，我关注着他在中国的事业和家庭，为他每次的成功和进步感到喜悦。在此，祝比汉家庭美满，幸福甜蜜！工作顺心，事业有成！

导师简介

彭翀，北航机械工程及自动化学院教授，博士生导师，全国自动化系统与集成标准化技术委员会物理设备控制分技术委员会委员。致力于研究数控装备可靠性、加工过程优化及网络化制造服务系统等。承担国家科技重大专项、国家自然科学基金、国家智能制造专项等 20 余项课题，如"基于部件退化动态耦合关系模型的数控系统多源信息融合可靠性研究"等。发表学术论文 60 余篇，开授先进加工技术及装备、制造工程基础——公差与互换性、数控机床加工动力学特性测试与铣削过程仿真优化实验等课程。

My name is Bilal Anwar, and I am from Pakistan. In 2010, with expectations for the future and thirst for knowledge, I bid farewell to my hometown and started on a journey to China. My destination was the prestigious Beihang University, where I completed my studies in Mechanical Manufacturing and Automation. On this journey, I not only achieved academic growth but also found a lifelong sense of belonging to this land.

Arrive in China: Experiencing Cultural Differences

Before arriving in China, my knowledge of this country was limited to some historical and economic data from textbooks. I knew that China was rising as a global economic and technological superpower, but to me, this unfamiliar land was still mysterious. Until I arrived in China in 2010 for the first time, Beijing had filled me with awe. With its towering skyscrapers, orderly traffic, and strong technological atmosphere, I felt both excited and nervous.

In the first month, I had to adapt to the huge cultural differences. Moving from Pakistan's city life to China's modern urban life, I felt I had entered a completely different world. My English was good but Chinese was the primary language for daily communication in China, and this made me feel at a loss at times. I decided first to grasp Chinese because I knew that language was the key to a new culture.

Fortunately, I started a year-long Chinese course. The course was well-structured, covering everything from basic pinyin and grammar to daily conversations. Gradually, I overcame the initial nervousness and unease, and I could communicate with classmates and teachers in basic Chinese. I remember feeling a special sense of accomplishment every time I greeted someone with simple Chinese sentences because I knew I was overcoming barriers and slowly integrating into this country full of opportunities.

Cultural differences were also a challenge. In Pakistan, our daily life is centered around social activities like family get-togethers and visiting relatives.

China also cares about family and relatives very much, yet efficiency and time management are more important. The fast-paced life in Beijing increased my stress. Both the crowded rush hour on the subway and the strict time management in the classroom made me realize I had to adjust my lifestyle to adapt to China's rhythm to obtain success.

Pursue My Dreams: Study at Beihang University

My dream was to become a mechanical engineer. After some surveys, I learned that Beihang University had a strong faculty and academic resources in the field of mechanical manufacturing. In 2011, I was admitted to Beihang University as an undergraduate in Mechanical Manufacturing and Automation. The beautiful campus and modern teaching facilities were a pleasant surprise. Here, I was exposed to cutting-edge technologies and participated in numerous challenging research projects.

The curriculum was tight and challenging, particularly in the field of mechanical manufacturing, where theoretical knowledge was closely integrated with practical application. Each hour of class study was not just confined to theories in the textbooks; it also included hands-on experience in the lab. I remember that in one robot control and automation course, my team designed and built a robotic arm capable of automatically performing tasks in complex environments. From design to implementation, every step was a challenge and allowed me to truly understand the wonders of mechanical manufacturing.

I took several courses that significantly influenced both my professional development. One of the most important courses I took was Mechanics of Materials, which covered all the characteristics of various materials. This course not only deepened my theoretical knowledge but also inspired my later research direction about Cold Stamping Die Design for Automobile Bodies. The most difficult course was Circuit Analysis. I sought additional help from professors, collaborated with classmates in study groups, and fully used the university's rich resources to understand the course content. These supports allowed me ultimately to excel in the course.

My undergraduate supervisor, Professor Xiufeng Wang, not only provided academic guidance but also showed great care for my career development. My thesis topic was Design of Advanced Car Bodies Using Sheet Metal Forming Methods. With her support, I had the opportunity to collaborate with engineers from BYD's R&D department, using SolidWorks and UG software to complete the design. Together with BYD, we designed advanced car bodies and conducted multiple physical experiments at their manufacturing plant.

During my graduate studies, Professor Chong Peng guided me into deeper research fields. He encouraged me to innovate academically and taught me how to integrate theoretical knowledge with practice. My master's research focused on Improving the Service Life of Aero Engine Gears Using Laser Shock Processing Technology. Throughout the research process, Professor Peng offered me opportunities to visit laboratories at Tsinghua University and collaborate with expert engineers. These experiences exposed me to internationally-leading research methods and technologies, enabling me to achieve academic progress while enhancing my practical skills. I also participated in numerous cutting-edge research projects, which boosted my confidence in the future of mechanical manufacturing and automation. One significant project I was involved in was the design and development of an autonomous drone control system, which required creating a drone capable of navigating complex environments autonomously. Together with my team, we conducted countless experiments and improvements, ultimately achieving a successful outcome.

During my time at Beihang University, I was lucky to join the student union, where I worked across various departments and gained valuable practical experience. From 2014 to 2015, I had the honor of serving as vice president of the Undergraduate Student Union. During my master's studies, I served as president of the Postgraduate Student Union. With the support the International School, we held a variety of extracurricular activities. For example, we organized sports competitions, cultural festivals, outbound trips to different cities, visits to state-of-the-art laboratories in China, and tours of historical and cultural sites. These activities not only enriched the students' experiences but also deepened their understanding of Chinese culture and technological achievements. Serving as the president of student union helped me learn valuable skills, such as team coordination, event planning, and cross-cultural communication. These skills have been instrumental in my professional career.

Cultural Integration: Life in China

As an international student, my life in China has been not only about acquiring knowledge and doing research but also about a deep process of communication and integration with the country. Beijing, with its rich history, is also a modern metropolis. In my spare time, I enjoyed exploring the city with friends. We visited historical cultural sites such as the Forbidden City and Temple of Heaven, as well as wander leisurely in modern shopping malls and high-tech exhibitions. China's technological development was extremely fast, and every time I visited a high-tech exhibition, I felt the immense strength of China's innovation in technology.

I also fell in love with Chinese cuisine. Particularly in the cold winter, I enjoyed going out to have hot pot with friends . The spicy taste always helped me forget the fatigue of the week.

Student Envoy: A Bridge of Friendship Between China and Pakistan

During my study in China, I witnessed the rapid development of China's economy. Particularly, after the introduction of the Belt and Road Initiative, I saw the immense changes brought to Pakistan by the China-Pakistan Economic Corridor (CPEC). CPEC has greatly promoted cooperation between China and Pakistan in multiple fields, such as economy, trade, and technology. From energy infrastructure construction to the upgrading of transportation networks, CPEC has brought unprecedented development opportunities to Pakistan. As a Pakistani, I am incredibly proud and excited because I see my home country benefiting from this great cooperation project.

I often followed the progress of CPEC. Whenever there were news updates about new projects being launched or major engineering milestones being completed, I would discuss these projects with my Chinese friends, reflecting on their significance for both countries. Especially in Pakistan, large-scale projects in energy and transportation have effectively alleviated local energy crises and traffic bottlenecks, improving the quality of life for residents. Before CPEC, we had a 12-hour power cut a day in Pakistan, but now our electricity is surplus, running our industry 24 hours a day. Thanks to the advanced highways built under CPEC, our goods from north Pakistan can now reach Karachi port within one day. I realized that as an international student, learning about China's advanced technology can also contribute to the cooperation and development between our two countries. I decided to stay in China, as I realized-and still believe-that as a Pakistani, I have a dual responsibility. On the one hand, I must give back to my home country and contribute to Pakistan's development. On the other hand, I hope to foster more communication and cooperation between the peoples of China and Pakistan.

Career Starting Point: My Beihang University Imprint

As a Pakistani student who has studied and lived in China for many years, China's rapid growth has left a profound impression on me, particularly in areas like infrastructure construction, technological innovation, and economic growth.

I clearly remember the first time I saw China's high-speed trains. Standing in Beijing North Station, I saw large crowds of passengers hurrying around the high-speed trains. The modern and streamlined design of the trains seemed to tell me about China's rapid rise in the transportation sector. China's high-speed rail network is now the largest in the world, connecting cities of all sizes and making travel more efficient and convenient. This infrastructure not only reflects the country's technological strength but also demonstrates the Chinese government's determination and efficiency in driving economic development.

In addition to transportation, China's progress in technological innovation is equally admirable. During my time at Beihang University, I experienced firsthand China's rapid development in areas like AI, 5G technology, and e-commerce. Whether in class or through discussions with classmates, I could feel Chinese students' passion for technology and their boundless imagination for the future. In my view, China's rapid development is not just about numerical growth and indicators, but it also represents the posture of a nation, presenting itself to the world.

I am deeply grateful for the high-quality education and abundant academic resources provided by Beihang University. Its rigorous academic atmosphere fostered my keen insight into technology and innovative thinking, giving me a significant advantage as I started my career. After graduation, I was fortunate enough to join SAIC Motors, a top company in automobile export. SAIC Motors focuses on intelligent manufacturing and automation, which aligns with my major at Beihang University. As an engineer, I was involved in the research, development, and implementation of several large-scale projects, such as establishing the MG Cars manufacturing plant at Lahore, Pakistan. Some of these projects serve the Chinese market but also extend to countries along the Belt and Road Initiative.

I am currently working in a Sino-foreign joint venture company. We manufacture automobiles in China and abroad. I apply the theoretical knowledge I gained at Beihang University to my work while also learning more refined and modern working methods from my Chinese colleagues. China's manufacturing technology is world-leading, especially in automation, AI, and industrial robotics. By participating in these projects, I feel incredibly proud, as I am not only a beneficiary of these technologies but also contributing to the technological cooperation between China and Pakistan.

In the future, I hope to continue leveraging my professional strengths to contribute more to the Belt and Road Initiative and the construction of CPEC. At the same time, I also hope to promote more China-Pakistan technological exchanges through my personal efforts. I believe that technological innovation is key to the cooperation between the two countries, and that education and talent cultivation form the foundation of this cooperation. Beihang University has given me a solid foundation, enabling me to advance in my career. I hope that more Pakistani students will come to China in the future, especially to top universities like Beihang University, to learn world-class technologies and knowledge.

Epilogue: The Unforgettable Years at Beihang University

Looking back on this journey, from the uncertainty and insecurity when I first arrived in China to now having a career and a family, I know that none of this would have been possible without the nurturing of Beihang University and the opportunities that China has provided me. Beihang University is not only my alma mater but also the most important turning point in my life.

Even today, I often think back to my time at Beihang University, those discussions in class with professors, collaborations with classmates in the lab, and the vibrant days on campus. These precious memories have shaped who I am today and guided my future path. I know that no matter how far I go, Beihang University and China will always be important home in my heart.

Messages from the Supervisor

Bilal is a handsome and generous young Pakistani man and also the first international master's student I supervised. When we first met, I was astonished by his fluent Chinese, his enthusiasm for learning and his love for China. And during our interactions ever since then, I have been increasingly aware of the shining points he possesses. Bilal is friendly, diligent, modest and optimistic. While achieving excellent academic results, he also served as the president of the International School Postgraduate Student Union. During the leisure time between busy and intense scientific research, we often had the chance to listen to him talk about interesting matters regarding how to coordinate and communicate with students from different cultural backgrounds.

After graduation, we have always maintained good contact. I have been paying attention to his career and family in China and feeling delighted for every success and progress he has made. Here, I wish Bilal a happy and harmonious family and a sweet and blissful life! May he have a smooth career and achieve great success in his work!

Introduction to the Supervisor

Chong Peng is a professor and doctoral supervisor at the School of Mechanical Engineering and Automation, Beihang University. He is a member of the Sub-technical Committee on Physical Device Control of the National Technical Committee on Standardization for Automation Systems and Integration. He has been engaged in reliability of numerical control equipment, optimization of machining process, and networked manufacturing service systems. He has led over 20 research projects, including the National Science and Technology Major Project, projects supported by the National Natural Science Foundation of China, and National Intelligent Manufacturing Project, such as the Research on Multi-source Information Fusion Reliability of High-end Numerical Control Systems. He has published more than 60 academic papers and teaches courses including Advanced Processing Technology and Equipment, Fundamentals of Manufacturing Engineering-Tolerance and Interchangeability, Testing of Machining Dynamics Characteristics and Simulation-Optimization Experiment of Milling Processes for CNC Machine Tools.

The "Feng Ru Cup" of
Beihang University Opens
the Door to Opportunities

13

北航 "冯如杯" 开启机遇之门

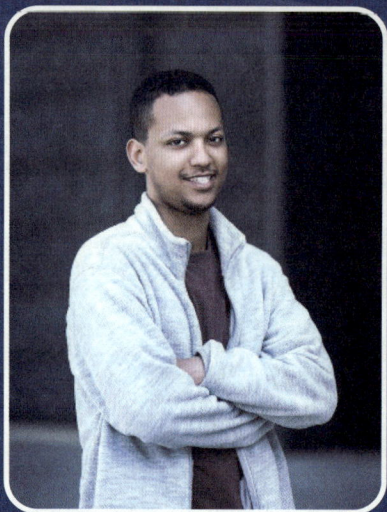

纳　尔

　　来自埃塞俄比亚的纳尔（Nael）于 2014 年带着自己的科技作品，跨越万里来到中国，参加北航的"冯如杯"科技竞赛。随后，他考入北航，完成了他的本科学习。2018 年从北航毕业后，他进入清华大学完成硕士学业，毕业后回国创办了企业 Chapa，提供处理数亿美元的支付网关服务，成为一位年轻有为的企业家。

　　Nael, from Ethiopia, journeyed thousands of miles to China in 2014, bringing along his scientific and technological works to participate in the "Feng Ru Cup" Science and Technology Competition held by Beihang University. Later, he was admitted to Beihang University and completed his undergraduate studies. In 2018, upon graduating from Beihang University, he entered Tsinghua University to pursue his master's degree. After graduation, he returned to his mother country and co-founded a company named Chapa, which specializes in a payment gateway service that processes hundreds of millions of dollars. He has since become a young and promising entrepreneur.

"冯如杯"开启梦想

我叫纳尔，2014 年我从家乡埃塞俄比亚启程，踏上了前往中国的求学之路，目的地是北航。这一切的起点是北航的"冯如杯"科技竞赛。

那时，我刚刚在埃塞俄比亚开始大学一年级的生活，内心对外面的世界充满了憧憬与渴望，渴望在更广阔的世界舞台探索未知、汲取知识。于是，我利用课余时间在互联网上搜索各类国际交流的机会，当我看到中国的北航举办"冯如杯"科技竞赛的消息时，我感到非常振奋。它不仅是一场大学生技能竞赛，更是一次能够让我了解世界、了解中国的宝贵机会。我坚信，参与国际竞赛，即便可能会失败，在这个过程中也可以了解到科技前沿动态，为自己的未来发展明确前进的方向。于是，我向北航"冯如杯"组委会提交了参赛申请。

可是，来中国参赛的旅程并不顺利。首先，我面临着一个现实的难题——交通费用。由于家庭经济条件有限，我无法承担从亚的斯亚贝巴到北京的机票费，一度陷入困境。但我不想放弃这个难得的机会，于是鼓起勇气给埃塞俄比亚航空公司发了一封邮件，说明了我的情况，并提供了参赛证明。我还记得，当时埃塞俄比亚航空公司邀请我和父亲一起去他们的办公室，也许是我的真诚和执着打动了他们，航空公司最终同意赞助我的机票，这才让我得以踏上这趟改变我人生轨迹的中国之旅。

那是我第一次来到中国。抵达北京，这座充满魅力的城市瞬间吸引了我。北航的校园更是让我眼前一亮。郁郁葱葱的青草地，优美安静的校园环境，现代化的教学设施，让我一下子爱上了这所大学。尤其当我置身于北京航空航天博物馆壮观的飞机陈列厅时，儿时心中对飞行的那份热爱瞬间被唤醒，我感觉梦想近在咫尺。学校为我安排了一名在校生志愿者帮助我。

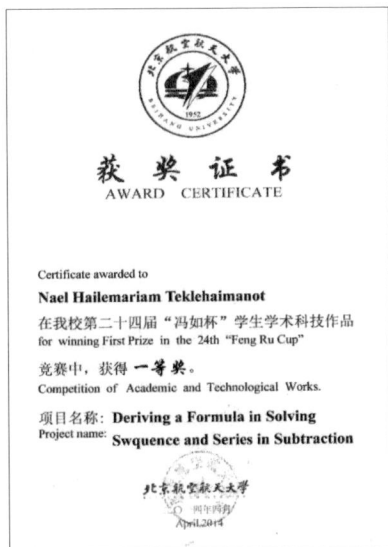

获奖证书

他帮我安排住宿，带我去食堂就餐，为我做语言翻译。这些贴心的安排和志愿者的帮助，让我在北航为期一周的比赛生活过得非常开心和轻松。我和他因此结下了深厚的友谊。这位同学目前在内罗毕从事建筑工作，我们至今依然保持着紧密的联系，经常分享彼此的生活与工作点滴。而我自己，也在这次"冯如杯"比赛中取得了不错的成绩，成为那一届比赛的一等奖获得者。这次参赛经历给了我很大的信心，也让我坚定了在中国继续深造的决心。于是我向北航国际学院递交了本科入学申请。

在北航的求学之旅

比赛结束后，我回到了埃塞俄比亚，迫不及待地向父母讲述我在中国的所见所闻。由于父母对中国了解甚少，一开始他们并不支持我的想法。我向他们展示了我在中国拍摄的照片，详细地介绍中国先进的科学技术、丰富的文化和北航浓厚的学术氛围。经过我的不懈努力，父母终于理解并支持我的选择。2014 年 7 月，我收到了录取通知书。2014 年 9 月，我再次踏上前往北航的旅程，开始了我的本科学习，主修电子信息工程专业。

到北航读书之后我才了解到，身边的中国同学都是经过中国高考的选拔，以优异的成绩进入北航的。能和中国的顶尖学生一起学习，我感觉自己充满了力量和干劲。在北航的学习生活中，我与中国同学的交流互动是我宝贵的经历。起初，文化差异确实给我们的交流带来了一些困难。我发现，中国理工科的学生在用英语交流时往往比较害羞，不太主动表达自己的想法。这让我有些困惑，甚至误以为他们性格内向。但我想真正融入这个学习环境，就必须打破这种隔阂。于是，我积极参与篮球运动，在球场上与中国同学一起挥洒汗水。作为一个团队，我们需要交流沟通，共同制订战术，彼此配合进攻防守。通过这种方式，我们逐渐熟悉起来，彼此之间的友谊也在不断加深。

我还主动与中国学生组队参加编程竞赛。赛前准备阶段，我们一起讨论问题、分享思路，共同攻克一个又一个难题。在这个过程中，我们的专业技能得到了提升，团队协作能力也变得更强，同时还结下了战友一般的友谊。

在本科学习的众多课程中，我最喜欢的是数字电路。我在这门课程上投入了很多精力，也取得了优异的成绩。后来，我还担任了这门课的助教。当我得知学弟学妹们对学习这门课程感到困难时，我用自己的学习经验告诉他们如何理解电路原理，如何进行电路设计和分析。在我的帮助下，许多同学都掌握了学习方法，也纷纷在这门课程上取得了不错的成绩。我还记得期末考试结束后，我们一起共进午餐。看到他们的进步，我感到无比欣慰，也更加坚定了自己在学习上不断前进的决心。

在中国的成长蜕变

除了课堂学习，我还积极参加各种实践活动，努力提升自己的综合能力。大二的时候，我偶然看到了一部介绍深圳的纪录片，片中展现的高新技术和创新氛围深深吸引了我。我毫不犹豫地向纪录片中介绍的公司发出了实习申请邮件。功夫不负有心人，我获得了一次宝贵的暑假实习机会。这次实习让我真正走进了深圳这座城市，亲身感受它的高速发展和蓬勃的创新精神。在实习过程中，我接触到了许多先进的技术和理念，对中国的科技产业有了更深入的认识。我还通过阅读相关图书学习了一些关于领导力的知识，进一步明确了自己未来的职业方向。

语言方面，汉语的复杂程度远超我的想象，庞大的汉字系统和独特的语法让我在学习过程中吃了不少苦头。但我没有退缩，我主动与中国人交流，积极结交中国朋友。在与他们的日常交往中，朋友们会认真地纠正我的发音和语调，帮助我理解那些晦涩难懂的汉字和词汇。同时，我还利用周末和假期的时间，游历中国各地。我去过哈尔滨，欣赏了美丽的冰雪节，感受了冰雪艺术的魅力；我到过河南的少林寺，领略了中国传统武术文化的博大精深；我漫步在西安的古城墙下，仿佛穿越回了古代；我走进了桂林的山水之间，陶醉于那里的自然风光；我还去了澳门，体验了中西文化交融的独特氛围。在这些旅行中，我不仅领略了中国丰富多样的地域文化，还结识了来自不同国家和地区的旅行者，与他们交流分享各自的故事和文化，进一步提升了自己的跨文化交流能力。

饮食方面，一开始我确实很难适应中国的食物。但我知道，要想真正融入这里的生活，就必须尝试接受这里的饮食文化。于是，我鼓起勇气尝试各种中国食物。慢慢地，我发现自己逐渐喜欢上了中国菜的独特风味，也习惯了用筷子吃饭。

　　本科毕业后，我前往清华大学继续深造，攻读数据科学专业。在清华的学习生活同样充实而富有挑战。我不断汲取新的知识和技能，为自己的未来发展打下更坚实的基础。在清华读研究生期间，我曾在腾讯实习，学到了很多专业知识和工作技能。

回国创业之路

　　在中国的学习与实践经历，尤其是在腾讯的实习经历，让我萌生了把在线支付基础设施引入埃塞俄比亚的想法。2020年，我回到家乡创办了自己的公司，名为 Chapa。这个词在埃塞俄比亚的俚语中是"钱"的意思。鉴于埃塞俄比亚人口的平均年龄为 19.5 岁，我

纳尔创立的公司

们期望打造一个能够引发广大年轻用户心灵共鸣的品牌。这是一个在线支付网关平台，旨在帮助企业便捷地接收在线支付。在埃塞俄比亚，很多企业在接收来自不同银行及各类电子钱包的支付款项时，面临很多困难。一般而言，要把所有这些繁杂的支付渠道实现整合，往往需要耗费两到三年的时间。而 Chapa 则扮演着支付聚合器的角色，凭借独特的技术与高效的运作机制，能够助力企业在短短 30 分钟内就顺利完成支付整合。目前公司已经运营了三年多，团队规模也在不断扩大，已经有大约 46 名员工。在公司发展过程中，我还与一位在中国结识的埃塞俄比亚朋友合作，我们相互协作、优势互补，共同探索新的商业机会。

致北航的国际学生

我想对正在北航读书的国际学生说：要积极和中国学生交流互动，而不是局限于国际学生的圈子。要尽可能地学好汉语，这将会为你的未来开拓更广阔的发展空间。此外，在学习期间要积极主动地寻找实习和实践机会，不断开阔视野，提升自己。

我在中国的经历是丰富多彩的，每一段经历都成为我人生中不可或缺的一部分。我深刻领悟到了勤奋努力的价值。同时，北航也激励我积极投身学生社团和校园竞赛活动。我在中国结交了很多朋友，和一些同学仍然保持着联系，我非常感谢北航的老师和工作人员，是他们让我能够接触到先进的知识和文化。我会永远珍惜这些回忆，继续努力前行，在自己的事业上创造更多的辉煌。我希望把自己的故事分享给更多的人，让更多的国际学生了解中国，我也期待有机会再次回到中国，与大家交流。

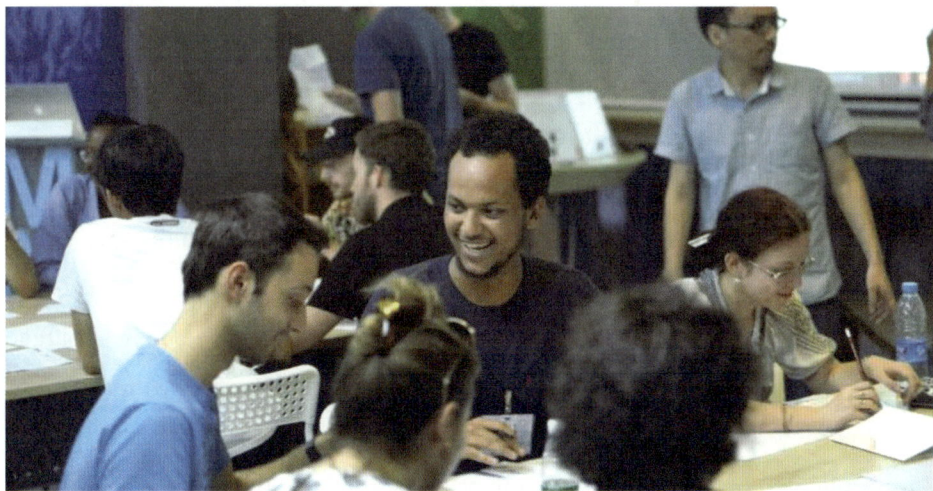

纳尔和同学在课堂上交流

The "Feng Ru Cup" Ignited My Dream

I'm Nael. In 2014, I left my mother country, Ethiopia, and embarked on a study journey to China, with Beihang University as my destination. The start was actually sparked by the "Feng Ru Cup" Science and Technology Competition.

At that time, I had just begun my freshman life at a university in Ethiopia. I was filled with longing and eagerness for the outside world. I was dying to explore the unknown and gain knowledge on a broader global stage. So, I searched online for various international exchange opportunities in my spare time. When I saw the news that Beihang University in China was organizing the "Feng Ru Cup" Science and Technology Competition, I was really thrilled. It was not just a skill competition but also a precious chance for me to get to know the world and China better. I firmly believed that even if I failed in this competition, I could still learn about the cutting-edge trends of science and technology throughout the process, thereby clarifying the direction for my future development. That's why I submitted my application to the organizing committee of the "Feng Ru Cup".

However, the journey to China to take part in the competition was far from smooth. I encountered a practical issue that I can't afford the travel costs. My family was smoothness at that time. I couldn't afford the airfare from Addis Ababa, Ethiopia to Beijing, China, and I was in a tough spot at that moment. But I wasn't willing to let this rare opportunity slip away, so I plucked up my courage and sent an email to Ethiopian Airlines, explaining my situation with the proof of my participation in this competition. I still vividly remember that Ethiopian Airlines invited my father and me to their office. Perhaps it was my sincerity and perseverance that worked. Eventually, Ethiopia Airlines agreed to sponsor my air ticket, which made it possible for me to start this life-changing trip to China.

It was my first visit to China. Upon arriving in Beijing, this enchanting city immediately caught my eyes. What impressed me even more was the campus of Beihang University, where lush green grass and shady trees could be seen everywhere. I fell in love with the university right away because of its beautiful and peaceful campus environment as well as its modern teaching facilities. Especially when I was in the magnificent aircraft exhibition hall of the Beijing Aeronautics and Astronautics Museum, the passion for flight that had been buried in my heart since childhood was instantly rekindled, and I felt that my dream was within reach. Moreover, the International School arranged a student volunteer to assist me. He helped me with accommodation arrangements, took me to the canteen for meals, and provided language translation for me. Those thoughtful arrangements and the great help from my volunteer friend made my one-week stay during the competition both pleasant and relaxing. As a result, I developed a deep friendship with him. He is now based in Nairobi, Kenya, working on building construction. We still stay in close touch nowadays and often share some touching moments of our everyday lives and work with each other. I also achieved good results in "Feng Ru Cup" and became one of the first-prize winners of that season. This experience gave me a great deal of confidence and strengthened my determination to pursue further studies in China. Consequently, I submitted my application for undergraduate study to the International School of Beihang University.

The Study Journey at Beihang University

After the competition, I returned to Ethiopia and couldn't wait to tell my parents what I had seen and heard in China. However, since my parents knew very little about China, they didn't support my plans to further my studies there at first. I showed them the photos I'd taken during my time in China, and gave them a detailed description of China's advanced science and technology, rich cultural heritage, and the vibrant academic atmosphere at Beihang University. Through my persistent efforts, my parents finally came to understand and support my choice. In July 2014, I was thrilled to receive the admission letter. In September 2014, I set off on my journey once again, returning to Beihang University to begin my undergraduate studies, majoring in Electronic Information and Engineering.

Upon arriving at Beihang University, I was well aware that the Chinese students around me had passed the highly competitive College Entrance Examination and entered with outstanding grades. Studying together with these top-notch students filled me with boundless energy and enthusiasm. I cherished interactions with my Chinese classmates during my study time, although at first cultural barriers did pose some challenges to our communication. I noticed that Chinese students majoring in science and engineering often seemed to be rather shy and didn't like to express their ideas when talking in English. This initially puzzled me, and I even wrongly assumed they were introverted. Yet I knew that if I truly wanted to fit into this environment, I had to break down these barriers. So, I actively played basketball games, sweating with my Chinese classmates on the court. Playing as a team, we had to communicate constantly, jointly devise strategies, and coordinate our offense and defense. In this way, we gradually got familiar with each other and our friendship kept deepening.

Moreover, I took the initiative to team up with Chinese students in a programming competition. While preparing for the contest, we brainstormed over problems, exchanged ideas, and overcame hurdles one after another. Throughout this process, not only have our professional skills been enhanced, our teamwork ability been strengthened, but a profound friendship has been developed.

Among all the undergraduate courses, Digital Circuits was my absolute favorite. I dedicated a great deal of effort to it and achieved outstanding results. Later, I became a teaching assistant for this course. When the junior students found this course difficult, I shared my own learning experience to help them understand circuit principles and conduct circuit design and analysis. With my help, many students mastered the learning methods and achieved good results in this course. I still vividly recall that we had lunch together after the final exams. Witnessing their progress, I felt an overwhelming sense of satisfaction and pride, further steeling my resolve to continue my studies.

Growth and Transformation in China

Beyond classroom learning, I actively engaged in various practical activities, striving to enhance my overall capabilities. During my sophomore year, I chanced upon a documentary about Shenzhen. The high technology and the vibrant innovative atmosphere shown in the documentary deeply attracted me. I sent internship application emails to the companies mentioned in the documentary. Eventually, I landed a precious summer internship opportunity. This internship allowed me to truly immerse myself in Shenzhen, experiencing firsthand its rapid development and vibrant innovative spirit. During the internship, I was exposed to many advanced technologies and concepts, and gained a deeper understanding of China's science and technology industries. I also learned about leadership by reading relevant books and further clarified my future career direction.

In terms of language, the complexity of Chinese far exceeds my imagination. The sheer number of Chinese characters and its unique grammar gave me a real headache during the learning process, but I didn't give up. I proactively reached out to Chinese people and actively made friends with them. In our daily interactions, my friends would painstakingly correct my pronunciation and intonation and help me understand those tricky Chinese characters and words. Meanwhile, I traveled across China during weekends and holidays. I visited Harbin, where I was mesmerized by the beautiful Ice and Snow Festival, experiencing the allure of ice and snow art. I went to the Shaolin Temple in Henan and was in awe of the profoundness of Chinese traditional Kong Fu. I strolled beneath the ancient city wall in Xi'an, feeling as if I'd traveled back to ancient times. I ventured into the mountains and waters of Guilin, completely intoxicated by the natural beauty there. I even made a trip to Macao and savored the unique blend of Chinese and Western cultures. During these travels, I got to appreciate China's rich and diverse regional cultures and met travelers from all over the world. We chatted together and shared our stories and cultures, which further honed my cross-cultural communication skills.

When talking about food, I struggled to adapt initially. But I knew that if I truly wanted to fit into life here, I had to give the local food culture a chance. So, I began to try all kinds of Chinese food. Slowly but surely, I found myself falling in love with the distinct flavors of Chinese dishes and also got used to using chopsticks.

Upon obtaining my bachelor's degree, I headed to Tsinghua University to further my studies, majoring in Data Science. The academic journey at Tsinghua was both rewarding and demanding. I continuously soaked up new knowledge and skills, striving to build a more solid foundation for my future. During my postgraduate study at Tsinghua, I joined Tencent as an intern, where I acquired a wealth of professional knowledge and practical work skills.

Return to Homeland for Entrepreneurship

The study and practical experiences in China, especially the internship at Tencent eventually led me to consider bringing online payment infrastructure to Ethiopia. In 2020, I returned to my hometown and founded my own company named Chapa. Chapa is a slang term for money used by Ethiopian youth. Given that the median age of Ethiopians is 19.5, we wanted to establish a brand that resonates with the majority of our users. It is an online payment gateway platform aiming to help enterprises receive online payments conveniently. Many businesses in Ethiopia face challenges when accepting payments from different banks and e-wallets. Integrating with all of them typically takes 2-3 years. Chapa solves this problem by acting as a payment aggregator, allowing businesses to integrate in less than 30 minutes. The company has been in operation more than three years, and the team size is constantly expanding, with about 46 employees now. During the development of the company, I also cooperated with an Ethiopian friend whom I met in China. We worked together, complemented each other's advantages and jointly explored new business opportunities.

To International Students at Beihang University

I have a few words for international students who are now studying at Beihang University: Actively communicate and interact with Chinese students, not just international peers. Learn as much Chinese as possible will broaden your future opportunities. Also, take the initiative to find internships while studying, keep broadening your horizons, and improve yourself.

My experiences in China were rich and colorful, each of which has become an integral part of my life. I have deeply realized the value of hard work, and Beihang University also encouraged me to be active in student associations and campus competitions. I made numerous friends in China, and I'm still in regular contact with some of my classmates. I'm truly indebted to the teachers and staff at Beihang University. They were the ones who helped me access advanced knowledge and rich culture. I will always cherish these memories, continue to work hard and achieve more glory in my career. I'm eager to share my story far and wide, hoping that more international students can get to know China better. I'm also looking forward to the chance to return to China someday to reconnect with everyone.

Nothing is Gonna Stop My Dream and Love for Beihang University

14

初心不改，北航情深

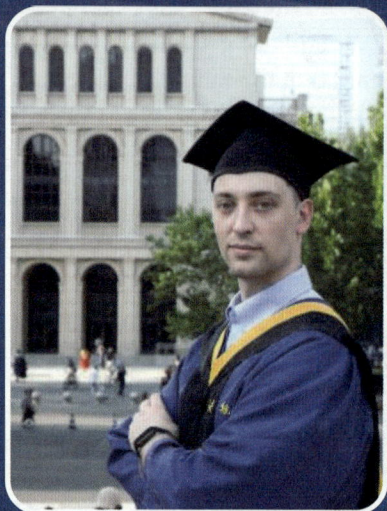

丹尼尔

　　Danil Dmitriev 是一名来自俄罗斯的校友，中文名为丹尼尔。2017 年，他通过国际暑期学校的活动首次接触到了北航，并对北航留下了深刻的印象。受此激励，他申请了北航的硕士研究生，于 2021 年 9 月至 2024 年 7 月就读于航空科学与工程学院，导师为朱秉钧副教授。毕业后，丹尼尔加入中国国有企业潍柴动力股份有限公司，担任应用工程中心的海外工程师。

　　Danil Dmitriev, an alumnus from Russia, came into contact with Beihang University through the activities of the International Summer School in 2017. Impressed by the university, he was motivated to pursue a master's degree at the School of Aeronautic Science and Engineering from September 2021 to July 2024, under the supervision of Associate Professor Bingjun Zhu. After his graduation, Danil joined the Chinese state-owned corporation Weichai Power Co. Ltd. as an expatriate engineer at the application engineering center in Weifang, Shandong Province.

学术启航

我是丹尼尔，一名以北航为荣的校友。2024 年，我获得了北航硕士学位。来到中国后，我被问到最多的问题之一就是如何适应中华文化。对我来说，这并不是什么挑战，我的父母在位于俄罗斯的一家中国公司工作，所以我从小就熟悉中华文化和中国美食。2017 年，在本科就读西伯利亚国立列舍特涅夫科技大学期间，我获得了参加北航国际暑期学校的机会。这次经历以及北航在航空航天领域享有的卓越声誉，燃起了我到北航攻读硕士学位的热情。

北航国际暑期学校部分学生合影

我从本科毕业前一年就开始准备申请材料，研究了北航提供的各种奖学金项目。我清晰地记得收到录取通知书的那一晚，以及随后确认获得中国政府奖学金的那一刻，我兴奋得彻夜难眠！

挑战与成长

在北航学习之初，我深入探索了一系列极具挑战性的课程，包括计算流体力学、飞机结构分析与设计以及航空航天材料概论。这些课程具有很大的难度，需要极其细致地关注每一个细节，并且深刻理解复杂的原理，特别是飞机设计相关课程。尽管面临挑战，我还是全身心投入，力求掌握这些知识，并利用观看录播课程、研读学术论文以及与教授和同学讨论等方法保证自己的学习效果。对我来说，最难忘的一门课是航空航天材料概论，课程将理论概念与实际应用相结合，极大地拓宽了我对这个领域的理解。

除了专业课程外，为了更好地与我的同学交流，我开始学习汉语，并在半年内通过了汉语水平考试（HSK）三级，我认为这是我在学术旅程早期取得的一项重大个人成就。回顾我的求学之路，由于适应新实验室的环境和要求需要时间，刚进入实验室时的我感到有些担心。然而，随着时间的推移和导师的指导，我逐渐获得了信心。北航完善的基础设施确保了我能够获取从试剂到设备等所有必需的资源，这帮助我在研究中不断取得进步。我的研究方向从本科时的飞行导航系统和飞机维修转向了人机与环境工程。这一转变使我能够参与前沿科学研究，包括生命保障和新能源系统在航空航天领域的应用。我的硕士项目与水电解制氢、制氧有关，对我而言，这个项目的主要挑战在于需要掌握跨学科的知识和技能。每周与导师的会面以及与同组同学的交流为我提供了宝贵的支持。在研究这一快速发展的领域时，

获评"优秀来华留学毕业生"

开始阶段我遇到的最大困难是跟进和分析海量数据。这个时候，我总是能够获得朋友和导师的帮助。在朱秉钧老师的指导下，我成功完成了硕士项目，并在毕业时荣获北航"优秀来华留学毕业生"称号，这也为我未来在中国能源行业的工作奠定了坚实的基础。

多彩生活

我积极参与各种学术和课外活动，这些活动拓宽了我的视野，增强了我的跨文化交流意识，并加深了我对中国传统文化的热爱。我聆听了多位杰出教授的讲座，他们提出了独特的见解，加深了我对研究领域不同方面的领悟。北航充满活力的国际学生社区提供了一个友好且富有启发性的环境。

此外，北航对科研和学术的重视使我能够参加工作坊和研讨会，进一步磨炼自己的技能，丰富我的学术经历，并使我有机会参与前沿项目。学校还组织了多次旅行和文化活动，让我有机会亲身体验这个国家丰富的历史。这些经历非常充实，我强烈建议同学们充分利用这些机会来拓宽视野。

我还很幸运地参加了其他一些活动，包括俄罗斯大使馆组织的活动、中国国际电视台（CGTN）和中国中央电视台（CCTV）的采访等，我甚至还参加了在著名的钓鱼台国宾馆举行的晚宴。

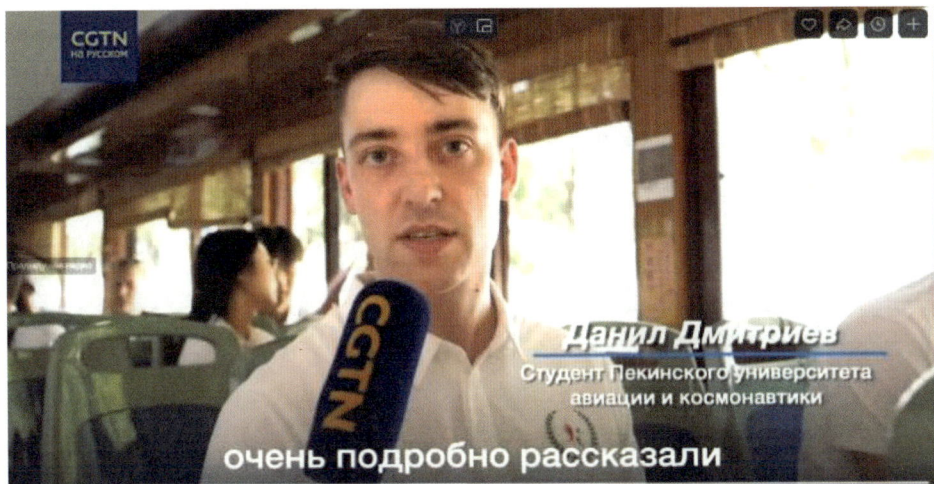

丹尼尔接受 CGTN 采访

丹尼尔（左二）参加晚宴

拥抱无限可能

对于在校学习的同学们，我的建议是：努力学习，充分利用在北航的时光，但别忘了去探索那些真正让你兴奋和激励你的事物。抓住在中国的机会，沉浸于中华文化中，迎接挑战，并尽力学习汉语。我鼓励你们毕业后考虑投身中国的发展建设。这个国家的众多行业在全球发展中处于前沿位置，

丹尼尔毕业后加入潍柴动力

融入其充满活力的发展环境，将为你提供在别处难寻的独特体验。要充分珍惜在北航学习期间所能享受到的教育资源和先进设施。

导师寄语

在收到丹尼尔的申请材料时，他在俄罗斯本科阶段优秀的学习成绩和获得的荣誉给我留下了深刻的印象。2017 年他通过国际暑期学校与北航建立的缘分，让他坚信北航就是梦开始的地方。研究生学习之初，他就向我表达了对中国的热爱以及将中国作为其事业起点的想法。丹尼尔在硕士期间对待学习和研究非常认真，同时积极参加各种国际交流活动。作为优秀俄罗斯国际学生代表，他受邀参加了"第三届中俄青年同走友谊路"活动，并参与了在钓鱼台国宾馆举办的启动仪式。他有幸被 CCTV 报道，并接受了 CGTN 的采访。毕业之际，丹尼尔被评为北航"优秀来华留学毕业生"，并如愿获得了在中国企业潍柴动力的工作机会，正式开始了他在中国的逐梦之旅。这是一条充满机遇与挑战，但拥有无限可能的道路，祝愿丹尼尔在这条道路上实现学生时代所畅想的中国梦，心系母校，不忘初心，坚持不懈，勇往直前！

导师简介

朱秉钧，北航航空科学与工程学院副教授，博士生导师。现任学院国际合作办公室主任。从事航空航天新能源和生命保障技术等相关研究。博士毕业于英国伦敦大学学院，博士后受"国际交流引进计划"资助任职于北京大学（获北京大学优秀博士后），在北航受"卓越百人计划"和"青年拔尖人才支持计划"资助任副教授。曾获国家自然科学基金青年科学基金项目和中国博士后科学基金面上资助，参与多项国家自然科学基金面上项目和技术开发类横向项目。在 *Advanced Energy Materials*、*Energy Storage Materials*、*Small* 等 SCI 收录期刊上发表论文 30 余篇，含 ESI 高被引论文 2 篇。

Academic Voyage

I'm Danil and proud to be an alumnus of Beihang University, where I earned my master's degree in 2024. One of the most frequently asked questions I receive is about my experience adapting to Chinese culture. For me, it wasn't much of a challenge, as my parents worked with a Chinese company in Russia, and I was already familiar with Chinese culture and cuisine from an early age. During my undergraduate studies at Reshetnev Siberian State University of Science and Technology, I had the opportunity to participate in Beihang University's International Summer School in 2017. This experience sparked my passion for pursuing my postgraduate studies here, as Beihang University is renowned for its excellence in the field of Aeronautics and Astronautics.

I started gathering application materials almost a year before graduation. I also searched for various scholarship programs offered by Beihang University. I vividly remember the night I received my acceptance letter, followed by the confirmation of my CSC scholarship. I could hardly sleep from excitement!

Challenges and Growth

At the beginning of my studies at Beihang University, I delved into a diverse range of challenging courses, including Computational Fluid Mechanics, Aircraft Structural Analysis and Design, Introduction to Aerospace Materials, and more. These courses were extremely challenging, as they required meticulous attention to details and a deep understanding of complex principles, especially in courses about aircraft design. Despite these challenges, I dedicated myself to mastering the class materials and leveraging resources such as recorded lectures, academic papers, and discussions with professors and schoolmates. One of the most unforgettable courses for me was Introduction to Aerospace Materials. This course combined theoretical concepts with practical applications, broadening my understanding of the field.

Apart from science and technical courses, I also began studying Chinese at

Beihang University to better communicate with my team members. Within half a year, I passed the HSK level 3, which I deemed as a significant personal achievement in my academic journey. Reflecting on my studies at Beihang University, my early days in the lab were stressful. It took time to reduce my anxiety and adapt to the environment and requirements. With time passing and the teacher's guidance, I gained confidence. Beihang University's excellent infrastructure, from laboratory reagents to equipment, from abundant resources in the library to rich dining options in cafeterias, made my daily life enjoyable and enabled me to access everything I needed for my personal life and studies, which helped me make consistent progress in my research. I transitioned from my undergraduate focus on flight navigation systems and aircraft maintenance to man-machine and environmental engineering. This shift allowed me to engage in cutting-edge research, including life support and new energy systems for aerospace applications. With regard to my research experience at Beihang University, my master's project is related to water electrolysis for hydrogen and oxygen production. To me, the major challenge of this project was the requirement of cross-disciplinary knowledge and skills. Weekly meetings with my supervisor, along with discussions with senior team members, provided me with invaluable support. Exploring this rapidly evolving field, navigating and analyzing the huge quantity of literature was particularly another big difficulty when I started my research work, but it was essential for staying informed and ensuring the success of each step of research. When encountering difficulties during my work, I always sought guidance from my friends and professors. Under the supervision of Bingjun Zhu, I successfully completed my master's project and was honored with the title of Excellent International Graduate Beihang University upon graduation, which laid a solid foundation for my future work in the energy industry.

Colorful Life

I was actively engaged in a variety of academic and extracurricular activities. I attended numerous lectures by distinguished professors, each offering unique insights and deepening my understanding of diverse areas within my field. Beihang University's vibrant international community provided a welcoming and stimulating environment. I established lasting friendships with peers from all over the world and took part in various cultural and academic events organized by the university. These activities broadened my horizons, enhanced my cultural awareness, and deepened my appreciation for Chinese tradition and culture.

In addition, Beihang University's strong focus on research and academic excellence allowed me to attend workshops and seminars that further honed my skills, enhanced my academic experience, provided me with the opportunity to work on cutting-edge projects and engage in hands-on learning. Moreover, I took full advantage of activities organized by the University to explore China. Excursions and cultural events offered me a chance to experience the rich heritage of the country firsthand. These experiences were incredibly enriching, and I strongly recommend students make the most of such opportunities to broaden their horizons.

I was also fortunate enough to participate in a variety of activities, including events organized by the Russian Embassy, interviews with CGTN and CCTV, and even a dinner at the famous Diaoyutai State Guesthouse.

Embrace Infinite Possibilities

My advice to current students at Beihang University is to study hard and make the most of your time there, but don't forget to explore what truly excites and motivates you. Seize the opportunities available in China, immerse yourself in the culture, embrace the challenges, and commit to learning the language. I encourage you to consider taking part in China's development after graduation. This country is at the forefront of global advancements in various industries, and being part of its dynamic ecosystem will provide you with unique experiences that are hard to find elsewhere. Take full advantage of the educational resources, expert faculty and advanced facilities.

Message from the Supervisor

When I received Danil's application documents, I was deeply impressed by his excellent academic performance and the honors he obtained during his undergraduate studies in Russia. His connection with Beihang University was established as early as 2017 through an international summer school, which further convinced him that Beihang University was the place where his dream would begin. At the very beginning of his study, he expressed his love for China and his dream of making China the starting point of his career. During his master's studies, Danil worked hard on his studies and research, and actively participated in various international exchange activities. As one of the outstanding Russian international students, he was invited to participate in the third China-Russian Youth Friendship Road event, attended the launch ceremony held at Diaoyutai State Guesthouse. He was reported by CCTV, and interviewed by CGTN. Upon graduation, Danil was honored as an Excellent International Graduate of Beihang University and successfully obtained a position at the Chinese state-owned enterprise Weichai, officially starting his dream-chasing journey in China. It is a path full of opportunities and challenges, with unlimited possibilities. I wish Danil could realize the Chinese Dream he envisioned during his student days, always remember his alma mater, stay true to his original aspirations, keep his perseverance, and advance ahead.

Introduction to the Supervisor

Bingjun Zhu is an associate professor and doctoral supervisor at the School of Aeronautic Science and Engineering, Beihang University. Currently, he serves as the Director of the International Cooperation Office of the School. He has engaged in research on aerospace new energy technologies and life support techniques. He got PhD degree from University College London, UK. After that, funded by the International Exchange Program, he worked as a Postdoc Fellow at Peking University, where he was awarded the Outstanding Postdoctoral Fellow. At Beihang University, with the support of the Outstanding Hundred Talents Program and the Young Top Talent Support Program, he serves as an associate professor. He has received fundings from the Young Scientists Fund of the National Natural Science Foundation of China and the China Postdoctoral Science Foundation Project. He also participates in several projects supported by the National Natural Science Foundation of China and industrial technology development projects. He has published more than 30 scientific papers indexed by SCI, such as *Advanced Energy Materials*, *Energy Storage Materials*, and *Small*, including 2 ESI highly cited articles.

Advance Knowledge
Frontiers and Bridge Cul-
tures for Global Careers

15

探学术研究路，跨文化职业桥

北京航空航天大学

托比亚斯·施图克勒

　　托比亚斯·施图克勒（Tobias Stückler）来自德国，于 2008—2013 年在慕尼黑工业大学（TUM）研究固体物理学。带着对知识的渴望和对成长潜力的追求，2014—2018 年，托比亚斯在北航电子信息工程学院取得微电子学与固体电子学专业博士学位，导师是赵巍胜教授。选择北航，一方面是因为北航与 TUM 有合作伙伴关系，另一方面源于北航的卓越声誉。

　　Tobias Stückler, from Germany, embarked on his academic journey in Solid State Physics at the Technical University of Munich (TUM) from 2008 to 2013. Fueled by curiosity for knowledge and the potential for growth, Tobias completed his PhD in Microelectronics and Solid-state Electronics at the School of Electronic Information Engineering from 2014 to 2018. His Ph.D supervisor is Prof. Weisheng Zhao. He chose Beihang University because of its partnership with TUM and its excellent reputation.

学在北航

2014 年"五一"假期的最后一天，我抵达北京，满怀期待地迎接新的人生篇章。第一次来到北航时，这所大学就给我留下了深刻的印象。校园面积很大，宿舍很多，周围还有许多商店和餐馆。同学们的热情和帮助让我倍感温暖。他们从机场把我接到北航，帮助我熟悉校园环境。初到大城市的紧张情绪，被同学们的善意极大地缓解了。

我在北航的学习时光因为丰富的课程安排而极为充实，课程包括专业课、数学课、汉语课和中华文化课。中华文化与汉语的学习非常有价值，它不仅对我的学术研究至关重要，也促进了我的个人发展，大大增强了我在新环境中的责任感和适应能力。

实验学习是我在博士研究期间的一个重点。起初，空旷的实验室让我不知所措，但我积极行动，逐步将其打造成我的工作空间。在老师们，尤其是赵巍胜教授的鼎力支持下，我采购了必要的设备并建立了测量系统。北航为我提供了许多难得的机会，包括与北京大学、电子科技大学、加州大学洛杉矶分校、惠灵顿维多利亚大学、洛桑联邦理工学院以及巴黎第十一大学等知名学校进行合作。

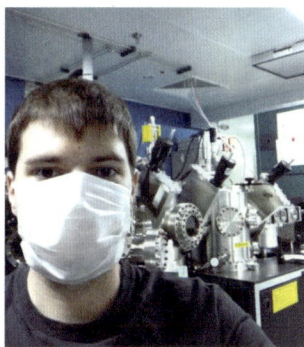

托比亚斯在实验室

我在科研中的高光时刻之一是有机会与诺贝尔奖得主阿尔伯特·费尔会面并进行讨论。我还多次在各地的学术会议上展示自己的研究成果，包括北京、青岛、柏林、牛津、圣迭戈和皇后镇等。我在国际知名期刊上发表了三篇论文，一篇发表在 *Physical Review B* 上，另外两篇发表在 *Journal of*

和诺贝尔奖得主阿尔伯特·费尔（右二）合影

Magnetism and Magnetic Materials 上，这些经历极大地增强了我的学术能力。

拼搏在北航

虽然顺利取得了上述成就，一路上我也遇到过许多挑战。文化差异和语言障碍考验着我的适应能力，而平衡科研与其他事项则需要细致的规划。不过，我通过自己的执着与分析性思维解决了这些问题。

为了应对文化和语言差异，我全身心沉浸到中国习俗和汉语的学习中。这不仅促进了我与同学间更好地沟通，也丰富了我的体验。通过主动融入周围环境，我建立了牢固的人际关系，这些关系在我应对复杂的新环境时起到了关键作用。

我遇到的另一个巨大挑战与我的研究相关，当我深入研究复杂课题时，常常在查阅相关的学术资源和数据库时遇到困难。为了克服这些困难，我采取了积极主动的

托比亚斯参加学术会议

态度。我与研究人员和机构建立了联系，为获取宝贵资源寻找通道。同时，我也向教授和同学寻求帮助，以更好地理解研究的细节。此外，我还参加了各种工作坊和研讨会，这不仅拓展了我的知识面，还让我从行业内的其他专家那里获得启发。

此外，我习惯于详细记录并分析遇到的具体问题。这种细致的方法让我能够厘清思路，为每个问题制定系统性的解决策略。面对解决方案中的机会与风险，我始终同等重视，并尝试做出明智选择。在克服困难的过程中，实施目标性措施起到了关键作用。

实验室团队合影

例如，面对事务性工作的挑战时，我制订了有条理的计划和时间表，以确保所有任务都能高效完成。通过设定明确的目标并跟踪进展，我能够在必要时调整策略。

我非常感谢中国同学、朋友和导师们的支持，尤其是于海明教授和赵巍胜教授的共同指导。他们的指导和鼓励在我克服困难时发挥了不可估量的作用。即使到现在，我仍不忘在北航受到的教诲与获得的经验，我与导师赵巍胜教授保持着长久的联系。

生活在北航

我的校园生活丰富多彩且充实。许多中国同学和朋友邀请我参加文化活动，这不仅丰富了我的体验，也加深了我对中国习俗的理解。我也结识了许多国际学生朋友，我们一起踢足球，还一起参加北航的足球比赛。

校园里有许多食堂、餐馆和商店，我记得有一家非常酷的理发店，它位于中国学生宿舍楼的负一层，是我的朋友介绍给我的。海淀区有许多大学，我参加过中国人民大学的烹饪课程，还去过其他大学学习汉语。我还找到了一位语伴，正是在这个语伴的帮助下，我的汉语水平得到了显著的提高，最终通过了 HSK 四级。

求职在中国

取得博士学位后，我很幸运地收到了来自深圳的博士后职位邀请，两家德国汽车公司也相继给了我工作机会。考虑到我的家乡是德国南部一个著名的汽车工业中心，所以我选择加入德国最大的汽车公司，就职于其位于北京的分公司。最初，我从事研发工作，如今已晋升为动力总成产品管理部门负责人，带领一个 5 人团队。我在北航学到的宝贵技能，为我从容应对工作中的挑战提供了助力。汽车市场变化快速，我每天都会面临压力，在传统汽车向新能源汽车转型的时期工作，是一件充满挑战的事情。工作之余，我仍然持续提升自己的汉语水平，并于 2021 年通过了 HSK 五级。

未来在世界

　　初来中国时，我计划在这里待三四年。如今，回顾在北京度过的 11 年，我非常感激当初做出来这里的决定。我取得了博士学位，开启了职业生涯，并成为行业内的专家和团队负责人。短期内，我的职业发展仍聚焦于北京，同时，我也在考虑中长期内搬迁到中国其他城市，甚至到世界其他地方。我从事的产品管理工作充满挑战且趣味十足，我会持续深耕。

　　当然，我希望进一步利用我的中德文化经验，促进跨文化合作，并在国际商业环境中创造价值。我的目标是在一家企业中施展专业技能，做出有意义的贡献，助力雇主推动创新。展望未来，我渴望承担更大的领导责任，可以是管理更大的团队，甚至是整个部门。除了实现业务目标外，我还致力于支持团队成员的职业成长，帮助他们提升技能并充分发挥潜力。

对国际学生的建议

　　对于那些即将踏上学术旅程，考虑在中国学习的人，我想分享一些自己在北航获得的宝贵经验。首先，学习汉语可以极大地丰富你的经历，并有助于日常交流。其次，如果

托比亚斯（右三）在博士论文答辩现场

有机会，一定要去探索中国令人叹为观止的自然景观。再次，最重要的是，为你的学习制订一个具体的计划。追踪自己取得的成绩，牢记未来要达成的重要目标，这对于在学术领域稳健前行至关重要。最后，记得保持条理并遵守北航的规章制度，如此你将获得一次顺利且充实的学术体验。

导师寄语

　　时光荏苒，转眼你已从北航博士毕业多年。回首你初到中国时对跨文化适应的忐忑，到如今在中德科技产业合作中独当一面的从容，我由衷为你骄傲。你将德国式的严谨与中国工程智慧相融合，在自旋电子领域的研究成果至今仍是实验室的典范。如今，你站在中德技术与产业合作的前沿，既是工程师，更是文化桥梁的搭建者。职场历练让你将学术理想转化为推动行业进步的动力，这正是博士培养的终极意义。望你始终保持探索的锐气，在技术创新中践行"知行合一"的北航精神。无论未来走向何方，请记住：真正的卓越，是让知识跨越国界，用合作创造价值。期待你继续书写中德科技交流的新篇章。

　　愿初心如磐，征途璀璨！

导师简介

　　赵巍胜，北航集成电路科学与工程学院教授，长期从事自旋电子学、新型信息器件及非易失存储器等领域的交叉研究。担任中国科协第十届委员会常务委员，教育部第八届科技委员会委员，工信部"空天信自旋电子"重点实验室主任。入选 IEEE Fellow，国家领军人才计划，获腾讯科学探索奖，华为奥林帕斯先锋奖，北京市自然科学奖一等奖，中国电子学会自然科学奖一等奖，中国仪器仪表学会技术发明一等奖等，是中国教师发展基金会首届卓越青年研究生导师奖励基金获得者。目前主持国家自然科学基金重大项目、国家重点研发计划等，近 5 年以第一或通信作者在 *Nature Electronics*、*Physical Review Letters* 等著名期刊和国际电子器件大会（IEDM）等顶级会议上发表论文 300 余篇，国际会议邀请报告 120 余次，专利超过 200 项。

Study at Beihang University

I arrived in Beijing on the last day of International Worker's Day vacation in 2014, filled with anticipation for the new chapter ahead. I was greatly impressed by Beihang University when I arrived for the first time since the campus was quite big. There were so many dormitories as well as a lot of shops and restaurants. The warmth and support I received from colleagues and fellow students were immediate and heartwarming. They welcomed me at the airport, helped me navigate my way around the sprawling campus environment. Their kindness effectively alleviated my initial nerves about moving to such a big city.

My time at Beihang University was enriched by a diverse curriculum that included scientific courses, mathematics, as well as Chinese language and culture studies. Learning about Chinese culture and language proved invaluable, not only for my academic research but also for my personal development. It significantly increased my sense of responsibility and adaptability in a new environment.

A significant focus of my research during my PhD was on experimental studies. Initially, the empty laboratory space was daunting, but I was able to take proactive steps to make it my own. With the incredible support from my supervisors, especially from Professor Weisheng Zhao, I assisted in procuring essential devices and establishing a measurement setup. Beihang University offered me remarkable opportunities, including collaborations with prestigious institutions such as Peking University, University of Electronic Science and Technology of China, University of California, Los Angeles, Victoria University of Wellington, École Polytechnique Fédérale de Lausanne, and the University of Paris-Sud.

One of the most memorable highlights of my research journey was the opportunity to meet and engage in discussions with Nobel Prize winner Albert Fert. Furthermore, I presented my findings at numerous conferences in various cities, including Beijing, Qingdao, Berlin, Oxford, San Diego, and Queenstown. I published three papers in renowned international journals, including one in

Physical Review B and two in *Journal of Magnetism and Magnetic Materials*. These experiences greatly enhanced my academic profile.

Strive at Beihang University

Although I have successfully achieved these accomplishments, I have also encountered many challenges along the way. Cultural differences and language barriers tested my adaptability. Balancing research with administrative responsibilities required careful organization. However, I tackled these challenges head-on through personal dedication and an analytical approach.

To cope with cultural and linguistic differences, I fully immersed myself in learning local customs and the Chinese language, which not only fostered better communication with colleagues but also enhanced my overall experience. By taking the initiative to engage with my surroundings, I cultivated strong relationships that were instrumental in navigating the complexities of my new environment.

One significant challenge I encountered was related to my research. As I delved into complex topics, I often faced difficulties when consulting relevant academic resources and databases. To overcome these research challenges, I adopted a proactive approach. I established a network with local researchers and institutions, which provided me with valuable access to resources. I also sought assistance from my colleagues and professors, allowing me to understand the details of the research. Furthermore, I attended workshops and seminars to expand my knowledge and gain insights from other experts in my field.

Additionally, I meticulously documented and analyzed the specific problems I encountered. This detailed approach allowed me to clarify my thoughts and develop a systematic strategy for addressing each issue. I consistently weighed the opportunities and risks associated with various solutions, and made informed decisions. Implementing targeted measures played a crucial role in overcoming obstacles. For instance, when faced with administrative challenges, I created structured plans and timelines to ensure all tasks were executed efficiently. By setting clear objectives and monitoring progress, I could adapt my strategies when necessary.

Thankfully, I received unwavering support from my Chinese colleagues, friends, and supervisors, especially from Professor Haiming Yu and Professor Weisheng Zhao. Their guidance and encouragement proved invaluable in overcoming these obstacles. Even now, the lessons and experiences I gained at Beihang University resonate with me daily, and I still keep in touch with my supervisor, Professor Weisheng Zhao.

Campus Life at Beihang University

My campus life was vibrant and fulfilling. Many Chinese colleagues and friends invited me to cultural events, enriching my experience and furthering my understanding of local customs. I also made friends with international students. We played football and even participated in a local football cup at Beihang University.

The campus has many different canteens, restaurants and shops. I remember a very cool hairdressing shop, a bit hidden in the basement of a dormitory for Chinese students, which my friend introduced to me. Haidian district has a lot of other universities. I attended some cooking classes at Renmin University of China and went to study Chinese at other universities. Additionally, I found a language partner who helped me achieve a commendable level of proficiency, allowing me to pass the HSK Level 4.

Career in China

Upon completing my PhD, I was fortunate to receive a postdoctoral offer in Shenzhen, as well as two competitive offers from German automotive companies. Given my roots in southern Germany, a renowned automotive hub, I chose to join the largest German automotive company in its China branch in Beijing. Initially, I started in research and development, and now I have been promoted to the Head of Product Management for powertrains, leading a team of five. The invaluable skills I learned at Beihang University have provided me with the ability to calmly face the challenges in my work, where I face the pressure of the rapidly evolving automotive market every day. I work in the transformative transition from conventional vehicles to new energy vehicles, which is very challenging. Outside of my work, I continued to improve my Chinese skills, passing the HSK Level 5 in 2021.

Future in the World

When I first came to China, my plan was to stay for 3 to 4 years. Reflecting on my 11-year journey in Beijing, I remain grateful for the decision to move here. I completed my PhD, started to work and became an expert and team leader in my field. In the short term, my career path still lies in Beijing, while I contemplate a mid-to-long-term relocation to another city in China or perhaps even a new adventure elsewhere in the world. My work in product management is challenging and interesting, and it's definitely a field I will stay in.

Additionally, I hope to further leverage my Sino-German cultural experience to foster cross-cultural collaboration and create value in an international business environment. My goal is to apply my expertise in a company where I can make a meaningful contribution, helping to drive innovation for my employer. Looking ahead, I aspire to take on even more significant leadership responsibilities, whether by managing a larger team or an entire department. Beyond achieving business goals, I am committed to supporting my team members in their professional growth, helping them develop their skills and reach their full potential.

Advice for International Students

To those embarking on their own journeys in academia or considering studying in China, I would like to share some valuable insights from my experiences at Beihang University. Firstly, learning some Chinese can greatly enrich your experience and facilitate daily interactions. Secondly, if you have the opportunity, exploring the breathtaking natural landscapes of China is a must. Thirdly, most importantly, make a concrete plan for your studies. Tracking your achievements and keeping your future milestones clearly in mind is crucial for navigating the academic landscape successfully. Finally, staying organized and adhering to the administrative requirements of Beihang University will ensure a smooth and rewarding academic experience.

Message from the Supervisor

Time flies. It has been several years since you graduated with a doctorate from Beihang University. Looking back on your initial anxiety about cross-cultural adaptation when you first arrived in China, to your current composure and ability to handle things independently in Sino-German technological industry cooperation, I am truly proud of you. Your research achievements in spintronics, which blend Germanic rigor with Chinese engineering wisdom, remain a model in the laboratory to this day. Today, standing at the forefront of Sino-German technological and industrial cooperation, you have evolved beyond being an engineer to become an architect of cultural bridges. Professional experience have enabled you to transform your academic ideals into the driving force for the advancement of the industry, which is precisely the ultimate significance of doctoral training. May you maintain your pioneering spirit and continue to practice Beihang University's motto of "the unity of knowledge and action" in your technological innovations. Wherever your path may lead, remember that true excellence lies in transcending borders with knowledge and creating value through collaboration. I look forward to your continued efforts in writing a new chapter in Sino-German scientific and technological exchanges.

May your original aspiration remain steadfast as rock, and may your journey shine with brilliance!

Introduction to the Supervisor

Weisheng Zhao is a professor at the School of Integrated Circuit Science and Engineering, Beihang University. He focuses on the interdisciplinary research in the fields of spintronics, new information devices and non-volatile memory. He is a member of the 10th Committee of the China Association for Science and Technology, a member of the 8th Science and Technology Committee of the

Ministry of Education, and the director of the Key Laboratory of Spintronics of the Ministry of Industry and Information Technology. He has been selected as IEEE Fellow, National Leading Talent Program and has won the Tencent Xplorer Prize, the Huawei OlympusMons Pioneer Award, the first prize of the Natural Science Award of Beijing Municipality. He has won the first prize of the Natural Science Award from the Chinese Institute of Electronics, the first prize of the Technological Invention Award from the China Instrument and Control Society. He has won the first Excellent Young Graduate Supervisor Award Fund of the China Teachers Development Foundation. Currently, he is leading some projects supported by Major Program of the National Natural Science Foundation of China and the Ministry of Science and Technology of China. In the past 5 years, he has published more than 300 papers in high-level journals including *Nature Electronics* and *Physical Review Letters*, and top conferences like IEDM. He has given more than 120 invited talks at international conferences and holden more than 200 patents.